THE DIARY
OF
Miss Idilia

THE DIARY
OF
Miss Idilia

Edited by
GENEVIEVE HILL

First published in Britain in 2010 by

Short Books

3A Exmouth House

Pine Street

EC1R 0JH

10 9 8 7 6 5 4 3 2 1

A CIP catalogue record for this book
is available from the British Library.

ISBN 978-1-906021-81-8

Printed in Great Britain by Clays

"Whoever dies before he dies
Does not die
When he dies"
Count Johann von Nassau

PROLOGUE

THERE ARE STORIES which, although long since forgotten, if told again can grip us just as strongly as they did those who first listened to them. This is one such story.

The scene of the story is the Rhine valley, which for as long as human memory extends has attracted people from every point of the compass. The English, particularly, have always travelled to the Rhine – indeed they discovered the valley before the Germans. One of the first to make the journey to the Rhine was Saint Ursula, daughter of the English king, who in 452AD together with her retinue of 11,000 virgins sailed up the Rhine to Basle, going on from there to Rome, where the object of their pilgrimage was to see the Pope.

English missionaries also favoured the pleasant travel

afforded by the valley of the Rhine. Arbogast, Pirmin and Wendelin came to these parts with the aim of converting the heathens, a mission later renewed by Lullus, Willisbrord and Suidbert.

In the 17th and 18th centuries, the Grand Tour – a tour of Western Europe – was seen by the noble and educated classes in England as necessary for the completion of a young person's education. One had to have seen the Rhine if one wanted to be considered a person of worth back at home. During this period Anglo-Saxon travellers – attracted and fascinated by the Gothic churches, castles and ruins, the crashing waterfalls, crags and battlefields of the valley – were a permanent feature of the landscape, and it is safe to say that the English developed a Rhineland romanticism long before the Germans did. A new trend grew up in England, the Gothic Revival – a current which came to influence architecture, art and literature.

The first English travel book appeared in 1783, entitled *Dreams, Walking Thoughts and Incidents*. The author was William Beckford, who described the Rhine valley as "the soul's landscape of dreams". In 1787 the Reverend John Gardner translated his impressions of the Rhine into drawings; from these 32 prints were made, which were included in a book published in London in 1791, *Views taken on and near the River Rhine*.

The years 1814 and 1815, following the raising of the continental blockade and the end of the Napoleonic wars, saw the advent of the age of mass travel. The world, tired of endless wars, sought refuge in romanticism; and once again, the English headed for the Rhine resuming the tradition of the "Continental Journey". In the spring of 1816 Lord Byron, journeyed there, and in "Childe Harold" he wrote lyrically of the river valley's landscape and history. This book was the first item the English Rhine tourists packed when preparing their journey; they loved all the places marked by decline and decay, all the monuments to transitoriness.

In 1817 Joseph Mallord, the most famous of all the artists who went to the valley to paint, returned home with a collection of sketches and 51 watercolours. In the same year the English steamboat *Caledonia*, owned by James Watt Jr, sailed along the Rhine as far as Coblenz, blazing the trail for the regular steamboat traffic between London and Mainz which started in 1829. Half of all the passengers on these boats were from England.

Over the next decade countless more works of literature and travel books appeared. 1832 saw the publication of William Tombleson's *View of the Rhine*, in 1833 *Travelling Sketches on the Rhine* came out, and in 1834 Edward Balwer Lytton's *The Pilgrims of the Rhine*. In the same year the English author Frances Trollope wrote "Like the farmer the rain, like the fisherman the shoal of herring, so the Rhinelanders await every year the arrival of the travellers from England". They were a frequent sight, as they traversed the valley with Murray's travel guide in their hands – the guide in fact which, with its conspicuous red covers, provided the model for the classic German traveller's handbook, the "Red Baedeker".

Not to be outdone, the English queen Victoria and her consort Prince Albert undertook a Rhine journey. In 1845 they visited a vineyard in Hochheim, the proprietor of which obtained permission to call part of his estate "König-Viktoria-Berg" – since when the English have regarded all German wine from the Rhine region as Hochheimer, or Hock. Of course, there were those who felt that this infatuation was exaggerated. In 1845, in *Legend of the Rhine*, William Thackeray took an ironic look at the Rhineland romanticism and Byronistic excesses of his compatriots. And some years later George Meredith published *Farina*, a pastiche in fairy-tale form of Rhenish legends.

But in the main the region was seen as an inspiration. Novelists found the landscape provided an ideal setting for the kind of macabre and fantastic story which came to be known as the Gothic novel (the forerunner of later days' horror and detective stories). The Rhine valley is an important presence in the most famous of all English Gothic novels, Mary Shelley's *Frankenstein, or the Modern Prometheus.*

And, after artists, nobility and royal personnages, in the middle of the 19th century a new kind of Rhine tourist appeared: the less well-educated English middle class, which had grown wealthy thanks to its enterprise and energy in trade and industry. Armed with sketch books, pencils and paintbrushes, in the best English tradition of the keen amateur, these new visitors produced drawings and watercolours of all they saw. They generally chose to eat, drink and sleep in the simpler, cheaper inns and village taverns. Among their favourite destinations, in addition to towns such as Cologne, Bonn, Andernach, Bingen and Mainz, was the old fortified town of Coblenz. And it was here that the Merchant William Dubb and his family – his wife Elizabeth and their children, Mary, aged 10, George, 15, and Idilia, 17 – came, from Edinburgh, in 1851.

Their journey ended in catastrophe, when Idilia disappeared one day, somewhere near the mouth of the River Lahn. Her tragic fate was finally explained some 12 years later in an article in the *Adenauer Kreis-und Wochenblatt* newspaper (No. 43, Sunday, 26 October 1863),

THE DEATH OF MISS IDILIA DUBB AT LAHNECK CASTLE, NEAR COBLENZ, IN 1851

Some of the number of our readers will perhaps recall that 12 years ago, all the newspapers of the Rhinelands, and subsequently of all of Germany, made great efforts to discover the whereabouts of a Miss Idilia Dubb, a lady who had inexplicably been lost to her family.

The English family, eager to enjoy fully the attractive landscape, had undertaken a walk to the mouth of the Lahn, spending the final night prior to Miss Idilia's disappearance in an inn in one of the villages of the region. Early in the morning the delightful young girl had taken her sketch-book, as was often her wont, and set off alone into the smiling summer morning.

At first, the fact that she did not return did not cause concern, since she was a passionate drawer, and whenever she found some beautiful countryside scene, she would not rest until it had been given a place in her sketch-book, even should this take half a day; consequently, it was not seen as a cause for concern that she did not return during the morning.

However, as evening approached without her having reappeared, her family, having now become worried, began to make enquiries. Initially these were not overly intensive, since her family felt that she had probably simply wandered astray, this being an area with which she was unfamiliar. However, when no sign of her was found on the following day either, it was clear that the situation was to be taken more seriously. The search for her was extended to all the newspapers of the Rhinelands, and subsequently of all of Germany; mountains and valleys, fields and woods, rivers and streams – no stone, it seemed, was left unturned, but still no trace of the missing girl was discovered.

It seems strange – indeed, one of those inexplicable and fateful circumstances which occur so often in life – that, in the midst of all this anxious seeking, scarcely a thought, if at all, was directed to the ruins of Lahneck Castle. The family of the missing person were, of course, strangers to the area, and those of the local population who had been out that way to look held it impossible that the English girl could have ascended the tower, since they had seen that the wooden staircase leading up into it had tumbled down and lay in splinters – and everyone seemed agreed that it had been in that condition for a long time. Thus it was that all the reconnoitring of the girl's parents, the people of the area and the police, all the rewards offered, all the appeals inserted in the newspapers proved fruitless. It was not even possible to conjecture what might have become of the unfortunate young lady – it was as if the earth had opened and swallowed her up, or some mythical creature had captured her and flown off with her, for, although one or two low voices were heard to mumble that she might have been abducted or fallen victim to some horrendous crime, nowhere was there the slightest indication that this could have been the case.

Nobody else saw Idilia Dubb after she left the inn. Nobody had seen any suspicious-looking person or noted any dubious circumstances; no shout had been heard, no drops of blood discovered, in no place was the

13

grass seen to be unnaturally flattened – in other words, there was no sign of any violent deed having been committed. All the anguished scouring of the countryside undertaken by the family, all their calling, questioning and weeping, were accompanied by the glittering sunshine of bright summer days, by the chirruping and warbling of the throats of a thousand birds, by the rustle of flowers and the splash of freshly springing water, the drone of beetles and the fluttering of butterflies: nowhere was any sign to be seen which might have furnished a clue as to what had happened, or awoken the searchers' suspicion.

After a long and fruitless period of searching and asking, the girl's unfortunate parents found themselves obliged to accept their fate and return home without their much-loved daughter. For months afterwards throughout the Lahn country the mysterious disappearance of the English girl was the subject of conversation, of conjecture and speculation – but with time interest in the episode abated, until it was forgotten.

The whole story would surely have remained in oblivion, had it not been decided a few years ago that it was necessary to dismantle one of the old castle's remaining towers, owing to its being completely decrepit. To the considerable surprise of those engaged in dismantling the ruin, at the top of the tower they found human bones. Nobody could explain how they might have come to be there, since, as we have seen, the stone stairway leading up to it, and later the wooden stairway which replaced it, had collapsed many years before.

This being such a strange and infrequent kind of discovery, the authorities in the area were informed; they directly appointed a commission, which was dispatched with instructions to investigate the matter carefully. The conclusions they arrived at were the following:

The human remains discovered in the tower were those of a woman, who had gone to her rest in a recumbent position, close against the rear wall. She had remained lying thus, exposed to the elements; with time some of her remains had moved from their original position. In addition, at one corner of the stone banister the remains of a white straw hat were found, and a short distance from this point marks made by the soles of shoes, a small gold watch on a chain, almost completely buried beneath earth and rubble, two rings, a small belt buckle, and a number of small clasps, which could be assumed to have belonged to garters.

The first question which presented itself was, naturally: Whose skeleton had been found? This gave rise to the second question: how had it come to be there?

It was while the first question was being pondered that the memory of the enigmatic disappearance of Idilia Dubb rose to the surface – especially when the doctor's examination concluded that these were the bones of a seventeen-year-old girl. Once the investigation had reached this point, the Prussian government found itself obliged to enquire in England after Mr Dubb who, according to the police registers of several towns of the Rhineland area, had travelled through these parts with his family in 1850 and 1851, with an English passport issued in Edinburgh.

It soon transpired that a man of this name had indeed lived in Edinburgh, but had died there in 1859. His widow, Mrs Dubb, when questioned, confirmed that she had indeed travelled through parts of Germany in the years in question together with her husband and their three children, and that close to the mouth of the river Lahn she had lost her eldest daughter in circumstances for which it had never proved possible to provide an explanation. Hereupon the widow was informed of the unusual discovery made in the tower at Lahneck castle, and when the objects found there were described for her she recognised them as having belonged to the daughter she had lost. In order to make sure beyond any doubt, shortly afterwards the unfortunate mother made the journey to Coblenz accompanied by her eldest son. She was shown the watch, chain, rings, buckle, clasps and other objects, and with stinging tears streaming down her countenance was able to confirm that it had all belonged to her child.

How, then, had the girl come to be in the tower? This was the second question which now begged for an answer.

The public were of course at hand with all kinds of horror stories. There were those who claimed that it had come to light that over a number of years strangers to the district had been disappearing, and that all the disappearances were in some way connected with the tower at Lahneck Castle. The tale went that a whole band of miscreants had carried on their doings at the castle, sometimes burying the victims of their horrendous crimes, sometimes hauling them up to the top of the tower on ropes so that the eyes of avenging justice could find no trace of them. If only a thorough search was undertaken, and the whole terrain dug over, then evidence of all kinds of atrocities would be uncovered.

The court was not to be swayed by such story-telling. For as long as anyone could remember, nothing worrying of this kind had occurred in the region. It was, moreover, out of the question that Miss Idilia Dubb had been made the victim of robbery. She had had no money with her, her mother said, and no items of value above the watch and rings which had been found together with her remains. What was more, no signs of any violence having been committed could be detected on the skeleton: the cranium and spine were in completely normal condition. In other words, she must have made her way up into the tower in some other, some voluntary, way; but how?

In the attempt to reach an answer to this question, certain considerations which thitherto had been disregarded, but were in fact of central importance, were brought to the fore. First of all, it seemed essential to establish up until what time it had been possible to ascend the tower. The stone spiral staircase, it was soon and unequivocally found out, had crashed down in the course of a storm in the spring of 1846, creating a cloud of dust and leaving nothing but a heap of rubble. However, since the tower afforded a delightful view far and wide over the Rhine and Lahn valleys, the following year a number of nature-lovers had had a wooden staircase built in its place, which had stood for years, enabling those who so wished to enjoy the captivating prospect.

In the summer of 1850, one or two voices were heard to say that the staircase had grown unsteady and was starting to crumble with rot, but witnesses said that it was still standing in May 1851. At the end of July of that year, it could be established beyond doubt, the stairs had been found to have tumbled down – and Idilia Dubb had gone missing in the middle of June. What, then, could be more natural than to assume that the unfortunate girl, tempted by the hope of gaining a view of the surrounding countryside, and being light of foot and unaware of any danger, had climbed the rickety stairs only to see them, as soon as she reached the top, crash down to the ground behind her? A reasonable assumption, indeed, but events were to transform this assumption into complete certainty.

For, when the coping of the tower wall was removed, a small diary was found to have been wedged into a gap in the mortar; its gilt-edged, partially mouldered pages were filled with Idilia Dubb's account, written in pencil, of the terrible fate which had befallen her.

Extracts of the original diary-entries were published in English newspapers, and subsequently appeared in the *Adenauer Kreis-und Wochenblatt* and other German newspapers.

The following presents the unabridged text of Idilia Dubb's diary from 1851 – slightly edited; one or two pages were missing, one or two pages were so badly decayed that it was impossible to read them. Certain additions have been made using the content of another, previous diary, which her parents had found in her travelling bags after she had disappeared.

1

Sunday, 8th June 1851

MY DEAREST GWENDOLYN, my one and everything and my soul's companion (I address you thus since the soul, like our friendship, is ever-lasting).

Nine months have now passed since you left Edinburgh, and with the exception of a post-card from New York, informing me that all is well with you, I have received no word from you. I know that, before you left, we agreed not to write letters but rather to each keep a diary to send to each other once a year, but I long to hear some news of you, and I do so hope that you will soon at least inform me whether you have now reached California.

I still remember well how strained we both were when you left. At the station, when I stood in the carriage door and called to you, I felt my heart would burst with the grief of parting from you.

Oh, Gwen, why did your parents of all people have to decide to emigrate to America, and why oh why did you have to accompany them overseas? You, who have been my best friend since we were five years old. We were going to conquer the world together, to win fame and admiration. How are we to achieve this now, when we are so far away from each other and are no longer able to encourage each other and keep each other's spirits up in times of dark self-doubt? Could not your parents, like my mother and father, have stayed in Britain and lived a modest but nonetheless good life, instead of going to America in search of uncertain fortune, and thereby putting also your future at risk?

Yes, I know that that sounds bitter and reproachful, Gwen – but in spite of what I say I envy you and your parents for having had the courage to take such a step, not fearing to leave your old life behind and begin a new one. I am certain that my parents would never be prepared to take such a risk, and if I am to be completely honest, neither would I. So now we must wait and see which one of us has chosen the right path, and which of us has chosen wrongly. One thing is clear, that if you had stayed with me in Edinburgh both of our destinies would have taken quite different turns – though whether for the better or the worse it is not yet possible to say.

Since our farewell at Edinburgh station I have had to make do with a portrait of you whenever I am overcome by the need to unburden my heart to you. You know the picture I mean: it is the water-colour which shows you wearing a straw hat, and your favourite yellow dress with the blue flowers on the edging, standing in front of an old stone wall. I am sure you remember it; I painted it last year, in May, when we went on that outing together with Genevieve to the ruin of St Anthony's Chapel, and Henry almost plunged from St Anthony's Seat with the horse and carriage. If only he had, I have often found myself thinking in recent days, then I would have been spared the disappointment of discovering him to be a faithless liar who did not love me, and to whom, to all intents and purposes, I meant nothing.

Yes, Gwen, I do of course recall that you and Genevieve warned me about Henry from the very outset; you told me that he was not suitable for me at all, and that in any event, as a nobleman he would soon start looking for a girl of his own station. But you also know that it was not my fault alone that this unfortunate connection came to be, that indeed most of the blame must be placed with my mother, since it was my mother who, in her conceit and ambition pushed me into a betrothal to Henry, knowing well that I felt no love for him. My father, too, is not without responsibility for this mistaken relationship, since he did not prevent Mother – who in her vanity sought to improve her social standing – from pairing me thus ignominiously with Henry.

However, I do not wish to apportion blame for the situation – I ascribe all responsibility to my young age and my inexperience, which I freely admit, in dealing with men. In future I shall certainly take good care to take no guidance other than that of my own heart.

In order not to expose myself to Henry's powers of persuasion, or to make it impossible for him to compel me to go back to him, I recently decided to remove myself from his reach by spending a period abroad, electing to accompany my parents and brother and sister on their holiday journey to the Rhine – this despite the fact that just a few days previously I had told them that I had no wish to make a second journey to Germany; for although I much enjoyed our first visit there last year, now I wanted to remain in Scotland to paint our own Scottish ruins rather than the ruined castles of Germany. Henry, who knows so much about historical things, was to be my guide, and show me the castles and country seats of his ancestors. Mother was of course delighted at this plan, seeing it as a sign that her daughter had at last come to her senses and begun to come to terms with her future role as a "lady of standing". Judge, then, how upset, how furious she was when I told her that I had terminated my liaison with Henry, and wanted to join my family on their journey instead. At first she refused to accept my decision, which she regarded it as utterly foolish, and she tried every means she could, going even so far as to beat me, to persuade me to reverse it. However, seeing that all her efforts were unable to overturn my resolution, she changed her tactics and resorted to pleading, begging me to return to Henry. When she realised that this approach, too, would not be able to sway me from my decision to break with Henry once and for all, she found herself obliged to give up, and even let herself be persuaded by my father and my brother and sister that I should be allowed to accompany them to Germany. She did, however, punish me, by treating me with icy silence and disdain for the whole of our railway journey to London, and also throughout our voyage in the steam-ship *Batavier* over the North Sea to Holland.

I wonder how long Mother can remain without speaking a word to me, and how long I shall be able to endure it. It is clear that George and Mary have already begun to find her behaviour irritating, and I can see that Father is made to suffer. However, I refuse to let Mother's coldness put me out of countenance; I can assure you that I have no intention of doing her that favour. Moreover, if there is someone here who should be the first to say something then it is Mother; it was, after all, she who started all this not talking.

I promised you, Gwen, when we said farewell, that I would keep a record for you of everything exciting that happens to me. Oh, if only I could tell you everything in person! Please forgive my poor handwriting, but I am half asleep as I write, just before going to bed, and the ship is rolling so heavily that I can scarcely write at all.

Last night I dreamt of the last ball I attended with Henry, before I had to take my leave of him for ever. In the dream I saw myself in my finest evening gown, surrounded by couples dressed in their finery, dancing with an elderly man in ceremonial uniform. We span around and around until I became quite dizzy. As the waltz slowed and changed into a calmer piece, I saw my fiancé hastening up the marble stairway to the first floor, where the black-haired daughter of the house stood in a door, smiling seductively towards him. On reaching the beautiful girl, Henry took her hand and disappeared with her into a drawing room, closing the door behind him after a final, furtive glance to see if they had been noticed. When I saw this, I tried to liberate myself from the arms of my dancing partner, but he wished to continue dancing with me. It was only after a deal of tugging and pushing that I managed to extract myself and, as he cast offensive expressions after me, make my way through the ranks of dancing couples. I reached the stairs, and ran up the broad marble steps, coming to a breathless halt at the door to the drawing room into which Henry and the girl had withdrawn. When I pressed on the door-handle, I found to my consternation that the door was locked. From within I could hear panting and gasping; and in order to ascertain whether my fiancé was indeed insolent enough to be unfaithful to me while I was in the same house, I ran into an adjacent, empty room. I opened the French door and, weak at the knees, stepped out onto the balcony. From there I could look into the neighbouring room, where, to my horror, I could see Henry and the daughter of the house lying in a state of some undress on the chaise longue, smothering each other with kisses. Shocked, I ran back into the empty room, rushed down the stairs and hastened towards the main door of the house, which a servant held open for me. Outside in George Street I stopped to catch my breath, and saw to my astonishment, on the other side of the street, the telescope shape of the Nelson Monument – which in reality, as you so well know, is on Carlton Hill, in a completely different part of Edinburgh. In my dream I heard a female voice calling my name from the top of the tower, and when I looked up I saw that it was you, standing on the platform at the top of the monument, calling to me and waving a portfolio of drawings. Overjoyed at seeing you again I hurried over to the tower and ran up the narrow spiral staircase inside it. When I reached the platform at the top I found to my great disappointment that you were no longer there; all I saw was my drawings, scattered around on the floor. I bent down to pick them up, and when I had picked up the last one, I suddenly heard your voice again, calling my name from what seemed to be a long way away. I leaned over the parapet and looked down, and there you were again, standing on the street waving to me, calling to me to come down to you as quickly as possible. Thereupon I swung myself over the parapet and, without a moment's hesitation, jumped, crying out "I'm coming, Gwen".

At the very moment I hit the grass below I awoke with a scream, and found myself in my cabin on the ship, lying on the floor having rolled out of bed as the vessel tossed in the heavy swell of the North Sea. I felt so afraid that my heart beat in time with the ship's engines, and it took a long time for me to become calm again. However, even though I was calm I was unable to go back to sleep. I lay tossing and turning in my narrow berth, listening to the stamping sound of the steam engines and my father's snoring from the other side of the thin partition wall of my cabin, and asking myself whether my nightmare was perhaps a bad omen for the future.

By early morning the monotony of the sea was finally behind us and we entered the Dutch port of Rotterdam. Moored there we saw gilded steam ships and tarred sailing vessels, decked with pennants and the flags of England, Prussia and Holland. My family and I, in comfortable summer clothes and weighed down with our luggage, left the steam-boat *Batavier*, together with other fellow passengers. The wind bore with it the tang of the North Sea, and the summer sun was busy dispelling the morning mist which lay across the harbour.

After spending a good hour standing waiting, without speaking and still tired from the voyage, among our mounds of packages and piles of cases, hat-boxes, umbrella covers and portmanteaus, we were finally allowed, at seven o'clock in the morning, to go on board our next vessel – a magnificent paddle steamer, the *Stolzenfels*, belonging to a Dutch steam-ship company with whom my father had reserved four cabins before we left England. The steamer, with pennants and flags flying, was to take us up the river Waal, which is a distributary of the Rhine, via Nymwegen and Cologne, to our first destination in Germany, Coblenz.

A great steam-ship like the *Stolzenfels* is something most impressive. Its motion is produced by two big steam paddles, which are driven by coal-fired steam engines. These engines create a terrible thunderous roar, as well as black smoke, which is discharged into the air through a large funnel situated in the middle of the ship. On the foremost part of the main deck coal and other bulky items are stowed, and to the rear an awning has been put up, to offer those passengers who wish to take the air protection from the weather. Below deck there are the passenger areas: there are three classes on board, saloon, large cabin and forecabin, and in addition there are a number of places in steerage for the less well-off.

After stowing all our effects in our cabins below deck, we returned to the main deck. We stood at the rail with other passengers, waiting for the boat to start the journey and watching the hustle and bustle of the quayside. Endless streams of passengers of every kind and description boarded our ship, until soon there was not a single empty space.

Two members of the crew were just about to pull in the gangway, when a piercing whistle from land halted them in their tracks. The shrill sound drew the attention of everyone on board to the person who made it – an elegantly dressed, good-looking young man, who held a suitcase in his left hand and a long clay pipe in his right hand. He was accompanied by two porters, who were groaning under the weight of a leather armchair which they were carrying between them. Seeing the three men coming towards our ship, the crew members pushed the gangway back onto the quayside, and with a firm voice the young man directed his two armchair bearers up onto the steamer. This gave us spectators the opportunity to observe the young man more closely, who for his part, despite our staring, seemed quite at his ease. He was aged in his twenties, and wearing a high, wide-brimmed hat. His suit had long tails and a narrow collar, bringing out the hips of the attractively built man and emphasising his shoulders. His waistcoat was open, and of a long cut; he had his shirt-collar turned down, and as he walked up the gangway I could see that his trousers were well cut. When he arrived on board and had his armchair placed on the main deck I could see that this attractive new arrival had blue eyes, and that under his hat he had quite long, dark brown hair.

Once he had paid his porters and they had left the boat, he settled comfortably into his armchair, lit his pipe and stretched out his legs to enjoy the view, thoroughly undisturbed by the gaping of his fellow passengers or their whispered, disparaging comments. Even my parents – who had been in a bad temper since our arrival in Rotterdam, and scarcely opened their mouths to speak – were unable to refrain from getting annoyed at the pampered young dandy in his leather chair. I too found his manner somewhat ridiculous at first, but I soon amended my opinion of him when I sat down on one of the wooden benches, and realised that my seat for the long journey ahead of us was much too hard and uncomfortable, and would surely cause me a degree of suffering. I now found myself thinking that the young man with his armchair was not in fact ridiculous at all; rather, he appeared to me as the wisest person on the ship, since he had arranged to travel in such a comfortable fashion. It is remarkable, is it not, Gwen, how quickly one becomes acquainted with strangers on a ship? I am sure you made the same discovery, when crossing to America.

Shortly afterwards the steamer cast off. On board and on the quayside hats were waved and tossed in the air, and from both sides people shouted their farewells. I observed the young man with the high hat talking briefly to the captain; and the captain then giving instructions to two sailors, who picked up the armchair and, accompanied by its elegant owner, carried it off in the direction of the foredeck.

The steamer kept to the middle of the river, churning through the water like a slow iron whale. It blew its smoke into our faces and whipped up a foaming surge on both left and right from which the spray flew, while beneath and beside us other steam and sail boats moved back and forth over the water.

My resolve on this morning was to put Henry's breach of faith and the frustration of the last few days behind me by devoting my attention to every aspect of nature's beauty, however small it might be. My eyes were to seek nourishment there, and my heart was to be filled with impressions. I had told myself that on this journey I would do a lot of dreaming, and a little thinking.

The mist was draped attractively over the river, which lay ahead of us, clear and green. Before long the sun had swept away the last whisps, which were replaced by small white clouds high in the zenith as the sky turned azure blue.

When a river has a strong current, to see it well one

must travel not downstream, but upstream, which is exactly what the *Stolzenfels* was doing. Every time we rounded a bend in the river we saw a small town, a village, or a hamlet, and above well-nigh every cluster where there were more than just a few houses there rose a windmill.

We passed a town with nineteen windmills called Kinderdijk. The name means "Child's Dyke", and a market woman on the boat explained to me that the town is called thus because in 1421 a baby in a cradle, still alive, was washed aland by a storm tide.

When travelling upstream one is constantly presented with new things to look at: a steam-ship bedecked with pennants, a small barque dancing on the waves, or a sailing boat tacking against the wind ahead of us. I held my hand up to shield my eyes from the sun and looked across to the bank, where young girls, of about my age, were stretching out sheets to whiten them in the sun, and a crowd of children – some of them completely naked, others wearing their shirts – ran after a flock of cackling geese. We passed picturesque cottages, where basket-makers sat in the doorway weaving baskets, and saw fishermen in their small crafts, mending their nets.

Towards the rear of the ship, on the afterdeck.We passengers sat under the awning on long wooden benches and at tables. We played boston, whist and other honourable card games, or sat with a glass of wine or lemonade and watched the flat lands of Holland float by, with their windmills, willow bushes and neat houses, while above us the June sun shone, unable to burn us for all its heat.

After so much sitting my back began to ache, so I rose from my place and strolled around the sundeck, observing the other passengers. The ship seemed to be carrying representatives of every social class and every temperament: a couple of the tables were occupied by raftsmen, others by rough market women who cluttered up the sundeck with their baskets of vegetables, causing not a few passengers to trip and stumble. At one table there sat five officers, wearing uniform and with unbuckled sword-belts, and at another three men who looked like teachers or professors. At yet another table two men whom I imagined to be statesmen or bankers were engaged in conversation, in the company of two elegantly dressed ladies of standing. In addition I saw tradesmen sitting next to their wooden cases, bird-cages and barrels of herring, students smoking long clay pipes, and a priest who sat leafing through a prayer book. Four waiters darted back and forth among the tables and benches, taking the passengers' orders. A large shaggy dog padded around, snuffling along the floor, leaving a trail of saliva behind it. From time to time a passenger would kick it, whereupon it gave a howl and trotted on to the next table, where within a short while it was accorded the same heartless treatment. To my relief, the owner of the dog finally appeared and put the dog on the lead, ending the poor animal's suffering.

A middle-aged man stood next to one of the ship's valves playing on a harp he had with him, to the tones of which his young female companion, who was wearing traditional folk dress, sang a melancholy song with a strong, clear voice – although the noise of the steam engines almost completely drowned them out.

Besides my brother George and sister Mary there were a number of other, mostly younger, children on board, who either hung anxiously onto their mother's coats, played with their dolls, building blocks or wooden horses, or careered wildly around the deck, an activity which earned them scoldings both from their parents and from other passengers.

The inside of the *Stolzenfels* was most tastefully fitted out, with the panelling and all the furniture made of mahogany. The food and drink were good and inexpensive, the four stewards who served us were quick and obliging, and no incidences of coarseness or brutal behaviour occurred on board. The needs of us passengers were seen to with such refinement that we could forget that we were on a ship, and believe for a while that we were out in the big wide world.

The prices of the meals on the *Stolzenfels* were graded in accordance with the passenger classes: they were most expensive in saloon class, cost a little less in large cabin class, and in forecabin class they were considerably cheaper. The cheapest meals of all were those served at the rear of the afterdeck, under the awning. That is where I sat, together with my parents and brother and sister, next to a middle-aged German man and a retired English army doctor, to eat *Oufbijt*, our Dutch breakfast consisting of dark rye bread, eggs, ham, cheese and honeycake. To drink there was tea or milky coffee. During breakfast the doctor told us that he had been travelling up and down the Rhine for years, and knew all the pleasant spots along the river, and almost all the different wines of the region. He found the stretch between Rotterdam and Düsseldorf tedious, and usually did not leave his cabin and emerge from below deck until the boat reached the town of Wesel, so he had only come up above deck now to have a cup of tea; after exchanging a little small talk with us he disappeared back into the bowels of the ship. The big German, with thick, black hair and bushy eyebrows, who introduced himself in rather poor English as being a wine-grower of the Rhine region, tried to engage me in conversation. I could not find him at all interesting and gave him the cold shoulder, whereupon he turned to my mother and began talking to her, while casting from time to time brief, furtive glances in my direction, which Mother did not however seem to notice.

On occasions the steamer pulled in at small towns and villages, and a signal shot was let off to inform the people living along the Waal of our approach. A ferry boat pulled out from the jetty, rowed towards the steamer, and then returned with one or two passengers to the shore, where men were waiting with wheelbarrows at the ready to receive the new arrivals and set off staggering and groaning under the weight of their bags and packages.

However comfortable the vessel, travelling by steamship is very tiring. In addition to all the noise generated by the boat itself, there is the running around of all the passengers, and the disagreeable, shuddering movements made by the ship, caused by the heavy engines and the great paddles. One would dearly love to creep into a quiet corner to get away from all of this, but there is not a single place on the whole ship where this is possible.

2

MY MOTHER, who sat opposite me at the table with a cold expression on her face, was still refusing to talk to me, so my father, who had grown tired of the bad atmosphere between us, made a clumsy attempt to reconcile us — although, owing to his inability to assert himself and to Mother's invincible stubbornness, he was unsuccessful. My brother and sister, who did not dare to talk to me for fear of incurring Mother's displeasure, kept silent, and sat looking straight ahead of them with embarrassed expressions and nervous twitching of their eyes.

At this moment I felt suddenly so weary of life, that I seriously considered throwing myself into the river in order to end it. I soon put the thought out of my mind, however, partly because I wished neither to set a poor example for my brother and sister nor to break my father's heart, and partly because I desired to show my mother that she could not get the upper hand over me that easily, that I do not have what she would regard as the weak character of an artist who is unfit to live. And anyway, you and I and Genevieve have made a pact, Gwen, to meet again in ten years' time to see which one of us three friends has achieved the greatest fame, and that is something I really do not want to miss.

Since I was unable to endure the oppressive silence at our table any longer, I finally stood up, picked up my sketch-book and rushed away, leaving my family behind, visibly surprised. I wanted to find some other place on the ship where I could at first rest to regain my calm, and then either write in my diary or make a drawing or two of the Dutch landscape. Finding no such suitable place on the over-crowded afterdeck, I decided to see what the fore-deck had to offer. When I reached the middle of the boat, where the bridge was located, I saw the captain and two helmsmen, spying out from their lofty lookout over the foredeck and the river ahead. The master of the ship, a big Dutchman with a sandy coloured beard, informed me that during the journey ordinary passengers were not allowed onto the foredeck, where coal and bulky goods were stored. When I gave him to understand that I only wished to make a couple of sketches of the river landscape he grinned, and called out to me in English "OK, I'll make an exception, seeing you're such a beautiful girl!" and allowed me to pass. A typical sailor – coarse and charming at the same time. I had already encountered men of his kind during the crossing from England, and found them intolerable, since I never knew where I was with them – whether they were taking me seriously, or whether they were just teasing me. I decided not to worry myself any more about the captain, although I knew very well that his eyes would be following every move I made.

I made my way onto the foredeck via a gangplank over the paddle-boxes, and immediately perceived that I was not the only visitor in that area, for there in the bows was the elegant young man with the leather armchair. I had forgotten all about him, with all the commotion on board. He was seated in the armchair, surrounded by chests, baskets and barrels, and since the back of the chair was pointing towards me I saw no more than the man's tall hat protruding above the back-rest, from beyond which white pipe-smoke rose into the air and was wafted over to me on the current. I was on the point of retreating to the afterdeck so as not to be seen by the young man – the last thing I wanted was to be drawn into conversation with him. After all, I did not know him; and I had no wish to make his acquaintance after all my experiences with men back at home. I was tired of their lies, indeed that was what had prompted my hasty decision to travel to Germany. I was just about to make an about-turn when I changed my mind, since it suddenly occurred to me that to walk away would have been tantamount to a capitulation. I wanted so much to sketch the river landscape ahead of the boat, and resolved to allow no man, with or without a leather armchair, to prevent me from doing so. At the same time, I did not want to give the impression that I wished to encourage the young man to establish contact with me by walking past his chair on my way to the bows to start drawing. So I took good care to remain behind the back of the chair, and stood at the side rail, from where I had a good view of the river and countryside ahead of the ship.

I had already made several pencil sketches of the landscape from various angles, filling several sheets of my sketch-book, when the man, his attention presumably aroused by the rustling of my sheets of drawing paper, suddenly looked round. On seeing me he smiled, and greeted me in German: "*Guten Morgen*". Since I do not speak good German, I replied by saying "Good morning". Knocking out his pipe he immediately changed tongues, and in the best English began to enthuse about the weather and the voyage. He then expressed an interest in seeing my drawings and surprised by the young man's friendly nature and never-ending flow of words, I agreed, after a moment's hesitation, to let him look briefly at them. I walked across to his armchair to show him, and he rose to his full length and extended his right hand towards me.

"Please, allow me to introduce myself: my name is

Christian Bach", he said, looking me straight in the eyes and pressing my free right hand firmly. I returned the introduction with "Idilia Dubb", my voice scarcely audible above the noise of the steam engines.

"It's so pleasant to make your acquaintance, Miss Dubb," he answered, bowing slightly. Thereafter Christian Bach, who was almost a full head taller than myself, let go of my hand and began looking with interest at my drawings. As he did so he uttered favourable comments such as "Yes, that's it exactly" and "Wonderful technique" while I, embarrassed by the interest accorded to my scribblings by a man unknown to me, was just waiting for an opportunity to escape from his flattering words and return as quickly as possible to the afterdeck. However, Christian Bach continued to comment on my drawings, and finally even invited me to take a seat in his leather armchair and resume my work. Before I could find a way of declining his offer he pushed me, gently but firmly, into the armchair, which, in comparison with the hard benches on the afterdeck, felt wonderfully comfortable. When he then placed my sketch-book on my lap, pressed my pencil into my hand and with a mischievous smile urged me to start drawing, I found myself no longer able to resist his charm. I remained seated and did what he said. You might think that this situation would inhibit my drawing, but on the contrary, I began to feel at ease in his presence, and although we had just made each other's acquaintance, it felt as if I had known him for much longer.

While I, with rapid strokes of my pencil, worked on conveying the river landscape onto paper, Christian sat down beside me on a wooden case and watched me. He told me that he himself would have liked to have been an artist, but unfortunately was not gifted, and so was only a commercial representative, who made his living selling mineral water in the Netherlands and London. In order to demonstrate to me the good quality of his water he opened his leather travelling bag, and took from it one of four small earthenware jars which were contained in a kind of leather case. He opened the jar and invited me to drink from it. It being a very warm day, and my mouth being very dry from all the talking I had been doing, I did not have to be asked twice, and took a small sip. The water was not cool, which I had expected it to be; instead it was luke-warm, although nonetheless refreshing, thanks to its slightly acidic taste. Christian explained to me that the water in the earthenware jar was what was left from a large consignment which he had delivered to Rotterdam a few days previously. When I expressed that I found it surprising that he sold water overseas and not the wine which is the usual drink exported from the Rhineland region, he answered that he did in fact sell wine in Holland and London, but only as a lure to get wholesalers on the hook, so that they would then buy his mineral water. I also asked the young Mr Bach where his water came from, and he revealed to me that it came bubbling out of the ground at a spring close to the town of Bad Ems an der Lahn, where it was bottled for dispatch abroad. This led me to tell him that, last summer, my family and I had visited the fashionable spa of Schlangenbad im Taunus, where we had drunk the "Bubbles of the brunnens of Nassau".

This information surprised my new acquaintance, and led us to tell each other something of our backgrounds. I learnt that he was 24 years old and unmarried, and that he originally came from the town of Oberlahnstein am Rhein but now lived in Bad Ems. In turn I told him that I was aged 17 and was still going to school in Edinburgh, and that my ambition in life is to be a painter. When I told the young man, in response to a question of his as to where my family and I would be staying during our sojourn in Germany, that we had taken rooms in an inn in Coblenz for three weeks, he seemed very happy and explained to me that Coblenz was only a few miles away from the town where he himself lived. However, before we were able to talk any more and discuss the possibility of arranging to visit each other, from behind me I heard someone calling my name, and when I turned around I saw George and Mary standing beside the bridge, waving to me to come. At this I realised that I had spent more than two hours on the foredeck, and that my family had certainly been wondering where I had got to. Not wishing to provoke even more annoyance with my mother, I immediately rose from the comfortable leather chair and gathered together my drawings. As I prepared to take my leave of Christian Bach, he held my arm to retain me and said "May I see you again, Miss Dubb?" I gave a forced smile and answered that I very much doubted that my strict mother would permit that, whereupon he smiled at me, and with the encouraging parting words "Don't worry, I'll make sure she does", let me go.

When I came up to my brother and sister they immediately asked me who the young man was and how I came to know him, at the same time casting curious glances in Christian's direction, who gave me a quick wave before sitting back down in his armchair. I answered their questions evasively, and learned from them that our parents had started wondering where I was and had finally sent George and Mary to look for me.

When we arrived back at our table and sat down, my father gave me a forced smile, while my mother took no notice of me at all, but continued her animated conversation with our neighbour at table, the German wine-grower, laughing loudly at his coarse jokes. I could see straight away that this was most embarrassing to my father, and also to my brother and sister. To put an end to the torment my brother summoned all his courage and asked Mother if he and Mary could go and stretch their legs around the ship, and to the great surprise of us all Mother, instead of giving her usual "No", allowed them to go. Happy to be able to escape, they jumped up and ran off, disappearing into the crowds of people on deck. I would dearly have loved to slip away myself, but for my father's sake I remained seated. The wine-grower's shameless flirting with my mother made him even more uncertain of himself than he is usually, and I could see from his expression that Father was racking his brains for the best way of extracting himself from what for him was an extremely humiliating situation without losing face or compromising Mother's honour. I tried to engage him in conversation in order to provide him with some distraction, but all his answers were disconnected, and his eyes kept returning to the other side of the table, where Mother was sitting. She is 43 years old, but she is still an attractive woman, which the wine-gower had clearly realised for himself, since his flirting with her continued unabated. Flattered by the attention she was receiving from the German, and with her face reddened by excitement and alcohol, my mother forgot her dignity and decency, and her loud laughter and the unrestrained familiarity she showed towards the wine-grower made her an object of ridicule among the other people sitting near us. The desperate attempts my father and I made to persuade her to show greater restraint came to nothing, met only with hard words from her side. This unpleasant situation reached a critical point when a steward arrived to take our orders. When Father, shaking with shame and uncertainty, asked my mother in a subservient and hoarse tone if she would like anything to eat or drink, she retorted in a cold, impersonal voice that she did not want anything. When he then made the mistake of trying to persuade her to order something, she snapped back that he ought to go and wash his ears since he was clearly having difficulty hearing. When she said this I saw the winegrower give a malicious leer and then order two cups of coffee from the waiter. Father, crushed by Mother's callousness, turned to me with deeply saddened eyes and asked me in a weak voice if I would like anything. I nodded, but before I could say what I wanted the steward had moved on. After a moment Father jumped up from his bench and, red in the face, rushed off in the direction of where the steward had disappeared, where he was swallowed up by the crowd. At first I felt like running after Father, but I changed my mind and remained seated, casting from time to time furious glances towards my mother and her German courtier in order to let them know what I thought of their behaviour. After a while Mother asked me in a barking tone why I was staring at her so stupidly; I answered that it was wrong of her to behave in such a way towards Father. At this she leapt to her feet and was about to slap my face, but the wine-grower restrained her, speaking to her to calm her down. Somewhat appeased Mother resumed her seat, but kept looking at me as if she would have liked nothing more than to strike me to the ground. For a moment I considered moving to another table, but when I saw that what Mother wanted most of all was to be alone with her conquest, I decided not to do her this favour, and stayed where I was. I tried to disturb them with contemptuous looks, but was unsuccessful in this since they both now ignored me completely, being interested only in each other.

The steward came presently with the coffee, and placed the two cups in front of the German. He pushed one of them across to my mother, who thanked him effusively. Irritated at the way my mother, who otherwise never behaved in an untoward manner in public, and far less showed her feelings to people she did not know, cast herself around the wine-grower's neck – in my presence, mark you – I felt like giving up and going to sit somewhere else. However, before I could do so my father returned to our table, carrying a tray on which I could see drink glasses and a plate on which there were a meringue and a cream puff. Father put the tray down on our table, and then stopped short when he saw the coffee cup in front of my mother. For a moment he looked as if he did not know what to do, but he quickly pulled himself together, and without a word put the plate with the cakes next to Mother's cup. When he then, visibly rendered nervous by the mocking looks he was getting from my Mother and the German wine-grower, made to give me a glass of lemonade, the glass slipped out of his hand and shattered on the deck into a thousand pieces. I could see from Father's expression that at this moment he felt so ashamed he wished the ground would swallow him up; I quickly bent down and started picking up the pieces of broken glass. Father, too, dived under the table to help me, dripping with sweat and bright red in the face. From here we could hear the wine-grower taking his leave of my mother, who apologised for "my husband's clumsiness". From our position under the table Father and I saw the German move off. When we stood up again with the pieces of glass in our hands, I saw that Father had cut himself badly and was bleeding from his thumb and index finger. While I immediately took out my handkerchief to try to stem the flow of blood, my mother did not lift a finger to help. I had a good mind to give her a piece of my mind, but could not bring myself to do so, owing to the stares of our neighbours and my fear of Mother's malicious temper. Father did not say anything either to rebuke her disloyality towards him, but remained standing in dejected silence, while I continued my efforts to stop the bleeding. These efforts were unsuccessful, and soon my handkerchief was completely red, and the blood was dripping onto the floor. Father, whose face only minutes previously had been as red as a beetroot, was now as pale as a sheet, and I was afraid that at any moment he might faint and fall to the ground. I took him by the hand and, followed by the curious looks of the other passengers, led him away from the table. I took him to his cabin under deck, steered him into bed, and put a bandage round his hand which finally stopped the bleeding. Shortly there-after my sister Mary came in, having heard of Father's accident from Mother. Mary was so worried that she threw herself in tears onto Father's chest to comfort him. I left Father in her care, determined to go and find Mother and ask her to kindly go and look after Father. However, when I unexpectedly bumped into her on the stairs up to the main deck this resolution evaporated; at the sight of her cold, hard face I simply stuttered "Hello" and then fled up the stairs to the upper deck, where I stood at the rail, relieved to have avoided a scolding or a hiding. With my eyes closed tightly I took deep breaths of the fresh breeze, to allow my nerves to relax.

I do not know how long I stood thus, perhaps it was for five minutes, or perhaps it was a quarter of an hour. Suddenly I heard a man's sonorous voice beside me, which roused me from my meditations. On opening my eyes I saw standing next to me at the rail, and smiling at me, a uniformed man with blond hair, of middle age. He had a moustache, and was wearing a round cap on his head and a sword at his side. His appearance led me to assume that he was a Prussian soldier, and when he saw the question-ing expression on my face and realised that I had not heard him he repeated himself, saying "Nice weather today" in English with a German accent, as if this opening phrase was so important to him that he felt obliged to say it again. At this the question crossed my mind as to whether the weather was the favourite topic of German men when they wished to strike up a conversation with a girl – I recalled that Christian Bach had taken the same theme as the subject of the first words he had spoken to me. However, in contrast to Christian, the Prussian soldier was direct and far less considerate. He took my hand, introduced himself as Adolf Wiessel, and then kissed my hand which, I must admit, rather threw me off balance. However, I kept my outward composure, in the belief that it must be the custom in Germany to greet new acquaintances in this way. I proceeded to introduce myself, at which the lieutenant used what to his ears was my unusual christian name as an opportunity to start flattering me and complimenting me on my looks. I was shocked by the lieutenant's forward manner, which repelled me – although at the same time it exerted an attraction on me. I was instinctively aware that this man could prove dangerous to me, but I nevertheless did not want to escape from his spell, so I let him touch me more than was really necessary, while with his intense stream of words he endeavoured to prepare me for touches of a less fleeting nature. I understood that in seeming to encourage him I was playing with fire, but my resistance was weakened as a result of my family problems – I felt a longing for someone who was strong enough to make me forget them, if only for the shortest of moments. That I might get into trouble with the lieutenant which would put my difficulties with my family in the shade was clear to me, but in spite of this I did not tell him to go to the deuce. On the contrary, I did not hinder him, and allowed myself to be more and more taken in by his ingratiating words.

The lieutenant told me of the tragic fate of a young Dutch girl called Johanna Sebus who, like me, was 17 years old "and very beautiful", and who, when a dyke burst, saved the lives of four people, pulling first her own mother and then another woman and her two children out of the river, before drowning in the flood water. He told me that Napoleon himself, impressed with the tale of the girl's selfless courage, had had a memorial put up at the place where the girl had lost her life. On hearing this story, I exclaimed to the lieutenant that it was most unjust of the Good Lord to thank the young girl for saving those people's lives by allowing her to die so young. In reply, Wiessel cited the saying "Those the gods love they gather early unto themselves", which I found very comforting, for although the young girl had lost her life, her good deed had made her immortal, which is a great mercy not granted to every human being.

The fate of the young Dutch girl gave me cause to think about my own future, and listening with only half an ear to the lieutenant I tried to imagine what my future life might look like. I wondered if my name would ever be inscribed on a memorial stone, and if it would, for what reason. I ardently hoped that I would one day be remembered as a famous painter and drawer – although I did not dare to indulge myself in such thoughts for too long, for fear of thereby steering my fate in the wrong direction.

I was not aroused from these musings until, behind the lieutenant's back, I saw Christian Bach climbing up to the bridge and talking to the ship's crew. I immediately realised that from his high vantage point he would soon see Lieutenant Wiessel and myself, and this was something I wanted to avoid at all costs. Although I found his company interesting, of the two men I preferred Christian Bach, since, he possessed a good portion of humour and self-irony, which were qualities that Adolf Wiessel appeared to lack, and which, in the final analysis, are more important to me than the kind of rough manliness exhibited by the lieutenant. I did not want him to be the cause of my relationship with Christian Bach ending before it had even begun, and so I decided to give Wiessel no more encouragement to continue his flirting. I interrupted him to say "I have to go now", and as I made to depart he held my arm to restrain me and asked, in a demanding tone, "But we will be seeing each other later, won't we?"

To this I answered, rather impertinently since I was irritated at his taking such a hard grip of my arm, that it was scarcely to be avoided on the ship. I then freed myself from his grasp. Taken aback by the sudden change in my mood, he looked at me in surprise, almost in disbelief. I left him and made my way through the throngs of people to the afterdeck, where I knew my brother George would be. My intention was to spend a brief moment with him and wait for a suitable opportunity to visit Christian Bach once more; I did not dare to go directly to Christian because then the lieutenant would have seen us and learnt of our acquaintance, and for the sake of peace on board the steamer I did not want him to find out.

When I reached the afterdeck I saw George sitting with his back towards me at the rail next to a large, fluttering Dutch flag, and looking out over the river. When I said his name he turned round, and on catching sight of me gave me a quick smile. I could see that he was still suffering as a result of all the bad blood with our parents, and would rather have been anywhere else than on this steam-ship somewhere in Holland. George is not usually the most talkative of people, and prefers to be silent rather than saying too much, but that afternoon it was as if a dam had burst: he poured out a flood of words which threatened to sweep me away. George had had enough, and much more than enough, of our parents' constant arguments, which they especially seemed to need to conduct in public, in front of complete strangers. He complained bitterly about our mother's hard and unforgiving nature, and our father's inability to assert himself against her. George said how much he was dreading spending three weeks with them in a foreign country. He reminded me of our first journey to Germany a year ago, when we children had to experience the shame of seeing Father, in an argument with Mother in an inn full of people, first allowing her to give him a thrashing, and then expose himself to still further derision by bursting into tears. My brother feared that this year things might get even more out of hand, and said that if this kind of embarrassing situation did occur again he might take to his heels and return to England by himself. I tried to talk him out of this adventurous plan, explaining that this was perhaps the last journey our family would make all together, but he replied that he "couldn't care less". What was more, he threatened to take our sister Mary with him on his flight back to England, so that she would be spared any further embarrassment on account of our parents. I told him that I did not want to hear such talk, and that as long as I was there, I would prevent him from executing his wild plan. George then started trying to persuade me to accompany them if Mother and Father should continue to have their tiresome arguments in public. Of course I refused to go along with this idea, but I promised him that when I had the chance I would have a serious word with our parents, in order to prevent our journey from turning into a horror trip, which is what George feared. Although I could see that he was sceptical, at length he agreed to listen to me, and said he would give up his plan to escape.

Happy that he had seen reason, I offered to buy him a lemonade, but he declined my offer. I saw him glancing at a girl sitting nearby, with fair, plaited hair, who must have been about 14 years old, and I understood why he did not wish to come with me. It surprised me that my brother should be so interested in a girl, since I had never before known him to be. Following my realisation, I did not want to disturb him any longer and hurried to leave him alone with his crush. I went quickly across to the table where our family had sat to eat, since I had left my sketch-book there. I took it under my arm, picked up my pencil, and made may way, through the masses of people sitting on the benches and walking around on the sundeck, towards the bridge. Once there, I saw only the captain and his two helmsmen; Christian Bach was no longer to be seen.

I looked all around, both to see if I could catch sight of Christian, and also to make sure that the Prussian lieutenant was not anywhere in the vicinity. I saw neither of the two men, so I walked on to the middle of the ship. Here I took the gangplank over the paddle-boxes, and came up to the captain on the bridge who, when he saw me, lifted his cap, screwed up his right eye and gave me a roguish grin. I replied with a friendly smile, and then left him behind me as I went out onto the foredeck. To my disappointment Christian was not there; all I could see was his empty leather armchair. I looked searchingly all around me, and was suddenly frightened by a signal shot. I discovered that the reason for this was that the steamer was approaching a landing stage. The jetty was filled with people, men, women and children, all of them with wooden clogs on their feet, who stood waving at the steam-ship with the smoke billowing out of its funnel.

3

A SHUDDER went through the hull of the mighty boat as it bumped up against the broad beams of the landing stage. Two crew members immediately leapt ashore with thick ropes and made them fast around two bollards. That done, they pulled a gangplank from the ship to the shore, over which a few passengers, laden with luggage, left the ship. Among them I espied Christian Bach, and seized by the thought that he was leaving the ship and that I would never see him again, I ran to the rail to shout "Goodbye" to him. However, when I saw that he did not have any of his luggage with him, I realised that he simply had some errand to carry out on shore and would be returning, so I did not shout, but contented myself with following him with my eyes until he disappeared in the distance, amid a crowd of people next to a big windmill.

I took up my sketch-book and, while waiting for Christian to return to the ship, began, using quick strokes of the pencil, to capture the hustle and bustle of the landing stage on paper. In the meantime some new passengers came aboard, laden like mules – big, fair-haired Dutch men and women dressed in their typical national dress their clogs clattering loudly on the deck boards.

With all the noise, which was added to by the cackling of geese on the shore and the noise made by the ship's steam engines, I had not heard that Lieutenant Wiessel had come onto the foredeck and was now standing behind me. I became aware of his presence when he cleared his throat noisily, and when I turned around and saw him there I almost fainted from fright. My reaction seemed to cause him some amusement, since he grinned at me, and was then also stupid enough to ask if he had frightened me. Before I could work out a suitable answer, however, he apologised for not behaving properly, so nothing became of the well formulated spiteful words I was thinking of flinging at him. On the contrary, I did not say a single word, since I was concerned lest Christian should return to the foredeck and find me standing there in the company of the lieutenant. The lieutenant cast a glance at my drawing and said he liked it, and then, on seeing the leather armchair, straight away sat down in it. At this I regained my composure, and told him to get up without delay, since the chair was the property of another passenger. At the same time I kept an uneasy lookout towards the shore, and to my consternation discovered Christian, walking rapidly towards the ship. In one hand he was carrying a wicker basket covered with a white cloth, and in the other he had a fishing rod. I could imagine what might happen if Christian found the lieutenant sitting in his armchair and me standing close by, so I once more admonished him to get out of the chair. Lieutenant Wiessel, who could not fail to notice my disquiet and clearly wondered why I was so anxious for him to leave his comfortable seat, refused to conform to my request. Far from doing as I had asked, he made himself comfortable and stretched out his legs, in order to illustrate to me that he had no intention of rising from the chair for a long while yet.

I decided to leave the lieutenant straight away, hurriedly closed my sketch-book and was just about to walk away when Christian came onto the foredeck and, happy at seeing me again, gave me a joyful smile. I gave a forced smile in reply, and before I could prevent him he placed his arm around my hips and steered me back to the foredeck where, without noticing the lieutenant in the armchair, he removed the cloth from the basket and showed me its contents, which, in addition to bread, cheese and fruit, also included two bottles of red wine, candles and a bunch of tulips. In response to my rather bewildered question as to what this all signified, Christian explained that he wanted to invite me to eat dinner with him that evening, adding in a mischievous tone, with a nod towards the fishing rod, that first he had to catch the main course. I of course found this a very amusing idea, but was unable to laugh about it because the lieutenant was still sitting behind us in the armchair, where he was keeping as quiet as a mouse and could hear everything Christian said to me.

I was just about to call Christian's attention to the presence of the uninvited visitor when he himself caught sight of him sitting there in the leather chair. I shall never forget the questioning look Christian gave me when he turned round to ask me how it was that this uniformed man had come to be sitting in his chair, with me standing so close. However, before I could stammer any explanation, Christian stepped up to the lieutenant, and after a brief "*Guten Tag*", pointed out in a friendly voice that it was his chair and asked him to get up from it. Lieutenant Wiessel showed no great interest in doing as he had been asked, replying instead that Christian should first prove to him that he was in fact the rightful owner of the chair. I could see how Christian stiffened at these words, but also how he restrained his urge to throw Wiessel straight out of the chair. Instead, he politely explained that the captain could confirm that the chair was indeed his property – whereupon Wiessel, nodding his head in my direction, provocatively asked if the same could be said of me, if I was his property too. Christian did not let the provocation ruffle him, but answered calmly that the lieutenant should leave me out of it and limit his remarks to Christian, if he was in such need of getting into a disagreement with him. Wiessel dismissed this, saying that since he was armed he would at any rate be the victor in any fight, and therefore had no wish to get his hands dirty unnecessarily. He then rose from the chair, and when Christian proposed that he should remove his sword so that they could settle the matter with their fists, the lieutenant gave a malicious grin and said that as a matter of principle he did not fight with civilians, since he always ended up giving them a hiding. He then made to leave, but Christian, whose self-restraint was all but gone, took hold of his sleeve to hold him back, and told him to stop being a coward and stand up to an honest fist fight. Lieutenant Wiessel merely looked down at the place where Christian was holding his arm, freed himself from Christian's grasp, and with a final look of contempt left the foredeck. To prevent Christian from working himself up into going after Wiessel and demanding "satisfaction" from him, I restrained him by the tails of his coat, and told him that if he really wanted me to have dinner with him he would have to stop being so ridiculous and looking for a fight straight away, otherwise I would decline his invitation. He then accused me of having been the cause of the argument, thanks to being acquainted with the lieutenant and having been in his company on the foredeck. At this I had had enough of Christian Bach as well, so I turned on my heels and left him, together with his leather armchair and his picnic basket, on the foredeck.

The steamer had got its speed up again when I reached the afterdeck, where the passengers were eating their mid-day meal. At one table I saw Lieutenant Wiessel sitting with four other uniformed officers. When he caught sight of me he looked in the opposite direction. Ignoring him, I walked straight past his table, and was just about to go below deck to my cabin when I saw Father, George and Mary sitting at a table in the far corner of the main deck. I made my way across to them, and Father asked me what I would like to have for dinner. However, after everything that had happened on board that day I had no appetite at all. I asked Father where Mother had got to; without a word he nodded in the direction of a table in the middle, where I saw Mother sitting with the German wine-grower, talking animatedly and with a bottle of wine on the table between them. I found the sight of my mother, shame-lessly carousing with another man in full view of her hus-band and children, utterly repulsive, indeed all but obscene, I felt sick. Giving as my excuse that I wanted to go and rest – but in reality not wanting to witness any more of the tragedy taking place on deck – I left Father and my broth-er and sister and rushed down to my cabin. I threw myself fully dressed onto my bed where at length, exhausted by all that had happened and the thumping of the ship's steam engines, I fell asleep.

I was woken by knocking at the door. Still half asleep I stumbled from the bed and opened the door, and was surprised to see Christian Bach standing there. "I wish to apologise for my stupid behaviour earlier on, Miss Dubb", he said in a remorseful voice, and did indeed really look sorry. He invited me to have a cup of coffee with him, but I declined his invitation, and said he should come back again a bit later. I then closed the door in his face, and lay down on the bed again.

At just after 2 pm I was woken by a signal shot, shortly after which I felt a heavy thud which shook the whole ship. I heard the slower beat of the ship's engines, so I knew that the *Stolzenfels* had stopped somewhere. When I came out on deck ten minutes later I saw that we were moored at the landing stage of a pretty town which, I learned from an elderly man, was called Nijmegen. I had read in my travel guide that together with Maastricht, Nijmegen was the oldest town in Holland. I had also read that in the 15th century there lived here a girl by the name of Mariken van Nieuwmeghen who, when she was 17, the same age as me, was tempted by the devil and fell under his spell. She followed the Evil One for seven years, before she repented and was able to free herself from his power. I stood at the rail thinking about this girl while my eyes roamed over the attractively decorated old houses and church towers.

After a short while I heard baying voices from the shore, and as I turned to look in the direction from which

64

the noise came I saw the four officers from our ship engaged in a fight with Christian Bach, while Lieutenant Wiessel stood by, observing the struggle with interest. Spurred on by some of the ship's passengers and a few onlookers from on shore, the soldiers struck at Christian, who with kicks and punches was desperately trying to ward off his assailants. He was already bleeding from his nose and mouth, and fearing that he might be killed in such an uneven fight I decided to intervene. I pushed and shoved my way through the crowds on deck and ran over the gangway onto the shore, where without hesitating I threw myself at the aggressors and in a furious voice ordered them to stop their cowardly attacks on Christian. My fearless intervention had the intended effect for the four soldiers did indeed desist, although not before one of them aimed a final kick at Christian's leg, which sent him groaning with pain to the ground. I leapt over to him to cover him with my body and defend him against any more kicks, but the soldiers had discontinued their attacks and gathered around Lieutenant Wiessel, who turned towards Christian and poured scorn over him for not being enough of a man to defend himself without the help of a young girl. Before Christian himself could say anything in reply, I shouted at the lieutenant that five men against one unarmed individual was not particularly manly, but was, on the contrary, a sign of cowardice and weakness. The uniformed men could not see the truth of this, but stood there smirking, saying stupid things and trying in every way to make Christian and me an object of ridicule. Only when he roared at them that each and every one of them was welcome, one at a time, to a duel with him, did they cease their abuse and retreat together to the steamer. Once on board they stood at the rail, grinning spitefully as, supporting Christian against me, I led him with difficulty up the gangway and onto the ship. Finding Lieutenant Wiessel blocking our way I pushed him so hard in the chest that he almost fell over. I proceeded to lead Christian, through the ranks of gaping onlookers, to the foredeck, where I helped him into his armchair and put a support under his aching legs. I then wiped the blood from his face with my handkerchief and gave him some water to drink from one of his jars. When I asked him how the fight with the soldiers had started, he told me that he had challenged the lieutenant to a fist fight on shore, in order to clear up once and for all the disagreement over the armchair. It had soon become clear, however, that Wiessel had no wish to fight for himself – he had four comrades with him who were to fight in his stead. This situation had not prevented Christian from having the foolishness to take on all four of them.

Since Christian had shown such a lack of sense in picking a fight with the lieutenant and his retinue I did not really feel at all like acting as his nurse, but I felt unable to refuse him my help, since he suddenly seemed so helpless and alone. So I took my handkerchief, wet it and used it to cool his face, which was hurting after all the blows he had taken. With my scarf I made a makeshift bandage and wound it round his knee, which was swollen from the kick the soldier had given him.

Having seen to Christian's needs I thought I would return to the afterdeck, but he asked me to stay for a while and keep him company, and I did. We watched as Dutch tradesmen came on board the *Stolzenfels* to sell foodstuffs such as fish, eggs, cheese and honeycake, and also Dutch tobacco, gin and geneva. Seeing all these delicious goods I suddenly felt hungry, and when Christian heard the rumbling of my empty stomach he took some bread and cheese out of his basket, together with a bottle of French red wine, and we sat together on the foredeck and had a little picnic.

Half an hour later the Dutch tradesmen left the ship, a signal shot sounded, the *Stolzenfels* steered back out into the middle of the river, and, lying low in the water and trailing black smoke behind it, once more started churning its way upstream. Christian and I watched the town of Nijmegen, with its towers and spires, disappear behind us into the haze. On turning to look ahead, towards the east, we saw that the sky was filling with black clouds. The weather had been close all day, and now it started to grow cool. More and more thunderclouds piled up above us, and by the wind we could tell that thunder was on the way. The steamer began yawing from side to side, and the sky darkened. Lightning flashed in the sky, and the distant thunder came closer and closer. Our ship, which could not go in to the shore owing to the low water level and the sandbanks in the river, rocked up and down on the swelling waves, and the captain and his crew had their work cut out to prevent it from capsizing. It started to rain, and when Christian and I walked over to the afterdeck in search of shelter, we found it completely deserted, with the exception of the harpist and his accompanying songstress, who were holding an umbrella over the instrument to protect it from the rain. All the other passengers had fled to their cabins below deck.

Since there were so many people on the lower deck, Christian and I sat on the spiral stairway leading down to wait for the thunder to pass. Indeed, the thunder was gone as suddenly as it had come, and soon the sun was shining above us again and the Waal once more flowed smoothly between its banks.

Christian and I dried off two chairs and a little table with our handkerchiefs, and sat down. A steward came and asked what we would like; I ordered a cup of tea, and Christian ordered coffee. Before long the other passengers started leaving the lower deck and returning to the main deck. I caught sight of my sister Mary, and called her over to introduce her to Christian. He gave her his hand and introduced himself, and the smile she gave him showed that she had taken an immediate liking to him. Mary seemed to make an equally favourable impression on Christian, and soon they were talking animatedly with each other as if they had known each other for much longer than just a minute or two. I almost felt as if I was not needed in their presence, although I was very happy that in Christian Mary had found an adult who took her seriously and listened to her, unlike Mother and Father who only listen with half an ear, and do not really take care of her since they are so preoccupied with their own problems. I myself, being only seventeen, am not yet mature enough to take the place of an adult for Mary, and George, too, at just fifteen and still too much of a child to be able to take the place of our parents.

The steward came with our drinks, and after Christian had ordered a lemonade for my sister the two of them resumed their lively conversation, which was about whether a steam-ship could be struck by lightning or not. During this time I kept a lookout for my parents, whom I had not seen for quite some time now, but to my relief I could not see them anywhere on deck. I assumed that Mother was in her cabin, sulking about something or other again, and that my father was busy trying to persuade her to make peace with him. However, I did catch sight of my brother, who was once more sitting next to the ship's flag on the afterdeck, casting longing glances in the direction of the object of his adoration, the girl with the plaited fair hair. I could not help smiling at the sight, but I immediately fell serious again when I saw my father stumble out onto the after-deck. His bright red face told me that he must have been drinking, and my experience told me that that meant that Father's attempt to bring Mother round had failed. Only too well could I imagine how she was lying on her bed in her cabin, thinking out ways of making life a misery for Father and us children. A shiver of fear ran down my spine at the thought that she could come storming onto the after-deck and make another dreadful scene with Father and us. However, my immediate concern was to prevent Father coming over to us in his drunken condition and making a fool of himself in front of Christian, so I turned my back in his direction and tried at the same time to screen my sister from his view. My efforts succeeded – my father did not see us, and made his way to an unoccupied table in the corner, from where it would be very unlikely that he would be able to see us. I breathed a sigh of relief as he sat down, although at the same time I felt ashamed.

The steward came with Mary's lemonade, and when Christian had paid him and he had moved off, I saw to my dismay my mother come out onto the afterdeck. In contrast to Father, she saw my sister and me straight away and headed straight for our table. Without greeting Christian, giving him only a suspicious glance, she asked me if we had eaten dinner yet. I made the mistake of saying that we had not done so, whereupon she told my sister and me to accompany her to another table where we would eat our evening meal. I tried to prevent this by saying that I was not hungry, and Mary, too, said that she did not want anything to eat, but Mother would hear nothing of it, and ordered us to go to the other table in a tone which allowed of no contradiction. I could see clearly on Christian's face what he thought of my mother's inconsiderateness, but he rose from his seat, and excused himself by saying that he had an important matter to attend to. As he left us with the words "Until later" and disappeared in the direction of the bridge, my mother said to me in a hissing voice that as far as that man was concerned there would be no "later" for me, since I had already spent far too much time dallying with him and in the future should look after my sister properly. I tried to protest, but my mother cut me off and ordered me to go and fetch my brother George, whom she had just located with her sharp eyes. I asked Mother if I should fetch Father as well, but she waved me brusquely aside and answered, looking over in his direction, that he could stay where he was.

When I went over to George, he at first refused to come with me, saying that the mere thought of having to sit at the same table as Mother gave him stomach ache. However, I managed to persuade him to join us at our late dinner, since he feared that there would otherwise be serious consequences for himself and for Mary and me. On our way back we passed close to Father's table, and I found it heartless that, just because he was drunk, he should be excluded from sitting and eating with us, so I went and asked him if he would like to join us. He did not need asking twice, and was happy that somebody should at last show some concern for him – even the steward, seeing that Father was drunk, had been ignoring him completely. Now Father trotted along after George and me like a devoted, faithful dog. Even at a distance I could see the hateful looks my mother was giving me for having dared to bring father to her table. However, at that moment I did not care what consequences my disobedience to mother might have, since my conscience no longer allowed me to see father suffering from Mother's heartlessness and lack of feeling. "Are you deaf, or don't you understand English?" she barked at me for having fetched Father, and then threatened me, saying "The next time you don't do as I tell you I'll throw you overboard!" Thereupon she turned to Father, who had awkwardly sat down at our table, and was staring down at the flowery tablecloth, for fear of meeting Mother's icy looks, which – as always in such situations – really were devastating, and would fill even the bravest heart with fear. "I don't want to hear a word from you, or I'll throw you off the table, do you understand?", she said intimidatingly to him, receiving a weak nod in reply. Mary's eyes twitched nervously and George was sitting completely motionless, avoiding making even the smallest movement which might attract Mother's attention and provide her with a pretext for dealing out complaints and harsh words. I too tried to make myself invisible to her by sitting absolutely still, but I did not succeed in my aim for, as she studied the menu, she continued criticising me fiercely for spending time with "that Prussian dandy", and promised that I would be severely punished if I had the insolence to talk to him again. My desire to see Christian again was strengthened still further by mother's stubbornness, and I longed feverishly for our next meeting.

Since father, contrary to what I had feared, kept quiet at table, and did not allow Mother's insulting remarks concerning his drunken condition and untidy state of dress to provoke him into starting an argument with her, the meal passed without incident, to the relief of my brother and sister and myself. On one occasion Mother was on the verge of starting a quarrel, when she thought that she herself should decide what we others should have to eat and drink. In order to avoid another scene we let her choose, and then obediently swallowed down the fish soup which she had ordered for us because it was cheap, and which smelt none too fresh. Our unappetising meal concluded with a sticky vanilla dessert, which was only just about able to take away the oily aftertaste of the soup. With the aid of several glasses of water my brother and sister and I finally managed to wash the stale fish taste away, although we could not wash it out of our memories.

Father almost fell asleep several times during the meal, and after paying the steward, Mother instructed me to take Father down to his cabin. I did not need asking twice, since it gave me the opportunity to escape from the oppressive silence which reigned at our table. I therefore took my time in taking Father to his cabin, and was not either in any hurry to leave it, but stayed for quite a long while with him, until at length he fell asleep.

4

WHEN I CAME up on the afterdeck I heard from other passengers that our ship had left the Dutch Waal and was now sailing up the German river Rhine, which lay before us, broad and mighty. Imagine: a river nine or ten times wider than the waters of the Leith at home in Edinburgh at its widest point; such an imposing sight and something I shall never forget.

We were sailing up the middle of the busy river, where sail and oar competed against each other. We saw every kind of vessel: a boat with two triangular sails and with its load stowed on deck, in a heap at the foot of the mast; a large raft with a wooden hut on it, and filled with raftsmen and sailors who plied their big oars in time with each other, thrusting them in and out of the water; a long tug-boat slowly pulling a string of heavy barges against the current, which the *Stolzenfels* overtook as it chugged its way upstream, not letting itself get distracted by the lively traffic on the river. On the horizon I saw, through a veil of haze, the outline of a town which, according to my guidebook, must have been Emmerich.

As I made my way back to the afterdeck I passed the five uniformed soldiers, who were sitting at a table with pewters of beer in front of them. Their tired eyes followed me as I went past. A moment later someone tugged at me from behind, and when I turned round I discovered that the hand that was holding me belonged to Lieutenant Wiessel. He requested an interview with me in private, but after what he and his companions had done to Christian I wished to have nothing more to do with him. This I explained in a few cynical, well-chosen phrases, before freeing myself from his grasp and hurrying off towards the table where my mother and brother and sister were sitting. On reaching them, I was astonished to see the three of them sitting playing brag together, and when Mother asked me to join in I agreed immediately and sat down with them, happy that she should suddenly be so sociable. Unfortunately, however, we children were not to have the chance to play cards with Mother and see her relaxed, even merry, for very long, for when her flame, the German wine-grower, appeared at our table and whispered to her to come with him, she dropped everything and followed

76

him. My brother and sister and I saw them disappear below deck, after which we lost all inclination to continue the game and sat without speaking at our table, hoping that Mother would reappear soon. However, the minutes passed, and she did not come back out onto the afterdeck.

When Mother had been gone for an hour George stood up, his teeth clenched, and went to sit at his usual place next to the ship's Dutch flag. He sat deep in melancholy on the rail, staring back in the direction from which we had come. Mary asked me, her voice marked by anxiety, if the man with whom Mother had gone below deck was going to be our "new father". This I refuted categorically, although in reality I was not at all as sure as I had made myself sound. On the contrary, recently there have been more and more signs that Mother is tired of Father and is constantly on the lookout for a suitable opportunity to put an end to their marriage. That said, not even in my wildest imaginings could I conceive that her current casual acquaintance, this German wine-grower who to my mind was a very dubious character, could be the one she would choose to replace Father. Indeed, I soon shook the idea aside, dismissing it as being far too improbable; I came to the conclusion that Mother, having grown weary of her marriage, had been looking for a holiday adventure, and found it straight away on the steamer, in the person of the Rhenish wine-grower. I felt certain that this liaison, as is the case with most holiday romances, would only last for a short time, and that afterwards Mother would return to Father, either filled with remorse or not. This thought provided me with a degree of consolation, since even if I did not begrudge Mother her little fling with the German, I really do not want her to make a definitive break with Father and make him, as well as myself and my brother and sister, unhappy.

While I was lost thus in reflection time flew past; it was not until a signal shot sounded from the ship's bridge that I was aroused from my meditations and realised that the *Stolzenfels* was approaching the town of Emmerich.

Ten minutes later the crew had made the steamer fast at the landing stage, and from the rail Mary and I followed with eager curiosity the busy comings and goings ashore, where, by a sentry box painted black and white, royal Prussian customs officials were inquiring of the passengers whether they had any dutiable merchandise. We watched passengers carrying their bags and packages back and forth over the gangway, and along the quays there were rows of wheelbarrows, onto which carriers were loading and unloading trunks, portmanteaus, packages and hat-boxes. The dress of the working population ashore was of the simplest imaginable kind: the men wore blue canvas trousers, linen waistcoats, jackets which came down to their knees, and blue spats with red garters; the women wore simple blue linen skirts, and on their feet they had clogs. As they regarded the passengers they seemed to have an expression of displeasure in their eyes.

The town of Emmerich was very decorative; there were unusual half-timbered houses displaying turrets and ornamental gables, their beams painted blue against the whitewashed walls. Outside the doors to the inns' wine gardens young women stood, trying to tempt the visitors by making a clapping noise with the lids of their wine pots. The river bank was filled with life: singing women were washing clothes, with children playing all around them; and swine and goose herds, armed with willow sticks, were kept occupied trying to prevent their animals from getting mixed up with each other. Strange smells were borne on the wind over to our ship, and when they reached Mary's nose she twisted her features in an expression of disgust.

Shortly after the customs officers had left the ship the obligatory signal shot was heard. The gangway was pulled aboard and the *Stolzenfels* cast off. The paddles churned up white spray from the river's green water, and soon the ship had got its speed up again and we were once more steaming upstream along the Rhine, where tranquil water meadows, old riverside castles, idyllic villages and beautiful small towns were waiting for us. Our next stopping point was to be the town of Wesel, where the crew and passengers of the steamer were to spend the night.

Not being able to see my mother anywhere on the after-deck, I resolved to defy her orders and pay Christian a visit. I took Mary by the hand, and made my way with her past the captain, who was standing on the bridge holding a shotgun, to the foredeck, where we saw Christian sitting in his armchair, holding his fishing rod and trying to catch fish from the river.

He was clearly very happy that my sister and I had come to visit him. He asked me whether my mother had changed her mind and allowed us to come and see him; when I said that she had not his expression became concerned, but I added in a self-assured tone that from now on I was not going to let her tell me what to do and what not to do.

At this point my sister clambered up onto the rail, and just as I was about to tug her back down I suddenly heard behind me my mother's loud voice, shouting my name. I turned round, and saw that she was standing on the bridge next to the captain. She gestured vigorously to indicate to me that I should go over to her straight away. However, before I could do so, I heard behind me a flock of squawking ducks flying up into the air, and at the same time saw that the captain had fired his shotgun. The loud bang from the gun was followed by a shriek from my sister, and as I turned round towards her, stricken with horror in the belief that the captain's shot had hit her, I saw her fall overboard. Seized with terror I rushed to the rail and looked over the side, and saw my sister in the water, crying desperately for help. Like Mary I cannot swim, so I was at my wit's end as to how to rescue her; however, even before

I had time to turn to Christian to appeal for his help, he had vaulted over the rail, and landed in the water with a loud splash. With vigorous strokes he immediately began swimming after my sister, who was drifting towards the ship's paddle and was in danger of being drawn into it and crushed to death. I could see the peril she was in and stood screaming with fear, as did my mother, who by now had come up to the rail and, her eyes wide with fear, was following the drama unfolding in the water beneath us. We heard the captain shouting orders in his loud voice from the bridge behind us, whereupon the beating of the steam engines grew quieter and the *Stolzenfels* reduced speed. Meanwhile we saw Christian reach my sister, who was half under water. He grabbed hold of her sleeve and at the very last moment managed to pull her away from the deadly paddle-wheel, just as she was starting to get sucked into it. The strong current dragged them both towards the stern of the ship. Mother and I both ran aft, and to our relief saw Christian, with Mary clamped under his left arm, holding with his right hand onto the end of a length of rope which a member of the ship's crew had thrown out to him. After what seemed to me an eternity of unsuccessful attempts, the crew member, assisted by three male passengers and using a boat-hook and all the strength the four of them could muster, finally managed to pull Christian and my sister on board. My mother and I were overjoyed to discover that although she was completely exhausted, Mary was uninjured. After we had embraced and kissed Mary, who lay on the deck, happy that she was still alive, and George had come to join us, his face as pale as death itself, it was Christian's turn to receive our expressions of gratitude for his heroic action. He had struggled to his feet and was busy wringing water out of his sodden clothes when I embraced him and said "Thank you for saving Mary's life", and even gave him a kiss on his wet cheek. My mother, who was clearly sapped of strength by the whole episode and had put aside her customary inaccessibility, then shook Christian by the hand and with a serious expression on her face thanked him, on behalf of herself and also of Father, for his courageous life-saving act. Christian, for his part, would hear nothing of all this, saying that he had merely done his duty, and then explained that he wished to go and change into dry clothes. He made his way through the other passengers, who were standing around us looking curiously on, and disappeared in the direction of the bridge.

I took Mary, who was crying softly to herself, by the arm and, accompanied by Mother and George, led her down the stairs to the lower deck. By now she had grown calm again, and I helped her to change her clothes. My father, woken by our voices, came into the cabin, and when he heard what had occurred in his absence was unconsolable at the thought that he had not been there to prevent Mary from falling into the river. I could tell from my mother's face that she felt like giving Father a telling-off, but she restrained herself, expressing instead her outrage at the fact that the captain had been so thoughtless as to practise duck shooting while sailing the ship, thereby endangering the lives of his passengers. For once I found myself in full agreement with my mother. Indeed, the more I thought about it the more incensed I became at the stupidity displayed by the master of the ship, which had nearly cost Mary her life, and I set off to the bridge to give him a piece of my mind.

On arriving at the bridge, my annoyment swelled still more when I saw a dead duck at the captain's feet, and saw the captain aiming his shotgun over the river towards where another flock of ducks was just flying up. At the same moment as I addressed the captain a loud shot went off, deafening me for a moment. Since the duck hunter had clearly not hit his target he spun round, his face distorted by anger, and started berating me. Owing to the bang, which was still echoing in my ears, I was at first not able to understand what he was saying, but after a moment or two I realised that what he was yelling at me was that I had no business being on the bridge. I paid him back in his own coin, and told him that because of his idiotic shooting my sister had nearly been killed. This made no impression on him: on the contrary, he now shouted that I had been on the foredeck with her although it was not allowed, and was therefore myself to blame for the accident. I retorted by reminding him that he had previously given me permission to go on the foredeck as and when I pleased, but all that I achieved by saying this was that he immediately prohibited me from going onto the foredeck any more. I found this completely unfair, for I wanted to pay another visit to Mary's rescuer who, as I could clearly see from the bridge, had had time to change into fresh clothes. He looked very smart, did Christian, in his blue tail coat, a flowered waistcoat, a white tie and straight-legged, rather narrow trousers which were turned up at the bottom. Unfortunately I was not granted any more time to admire him, for the captain stretched out his arm, pointing towards the afterdeck, and told me bluntly to get my "English backside" over there straight away and keep it stuck on the bench for the rest of the journey. I gave him a look of contempt, called out to Christian to attract his attention, and then retreated to the afterdeck. As I expected he appeared next to me a moment later; when I told him about the captain's ban he answered that there was no need for me to take it too much to heart, since he could just as easily spend his time with me on the afterdeck. I agreed with him, and when I said he should go and fetch his armchair he said that it was not worthwhile, since the *Stolzenfels* would anyway soon be reaching Wesel.

The sun was just going down in the west as the steamer approached the old Hanseatic town where, following some very time-consuming manoeuvring through a narrow, silted-up channel, it could finally moor at its night-time stopping point alongside the river bank. From the bridge the captain shouted out "We've arrived!", as if we passengers had not realised that fact a good while before. All the passengers on board stood up, either in order to go ashore or to make their way to their cabins below deck.

Before us lay the vast grounds of a fortress, behind which we could see the silhouette of the town with its turrets, gables, church towers and the imposing St Willibrord cathedral. This historical town inspired in us passengers a feeling of reverence, and while we waited for the deck to empty I became lost in contemplation, seeming to feel the spirit of the centuries brushing over me. We were in a land of legend and saga, where everywhere one comes across places which are the scene of fairy-tales and horror stories, and where every fallen stone and grain of sand has a story of its own to tell.

The evening in Wesel was uncommonly mild. In the distance I could hear church bells tolling, the hammering of a blacksmith on an anvil, and an officer shouting orders in the fortress. Singing washerwomen, with baskets full of laundry on their heads, were on their way home, heading towards the gate in the town wall. There was a wooden pontoon bridge across the Rhine, and on the other bank I saw two horses on a towpath, pulling a sailing boat with triangular sails slowly upstream. The stamping hooves of the pair of horses, the jingling of their bells and the cracking of the towman's whip carried across to our ship.

Christian had not taken a cabin; he told me that he never did on his travels, so he intended to spend the night in an inn in Wesel. He invited me to go for a walk with him so that he could show me the town, which he knew well since he often stayed within its walls. However I expected that my parents would want to go into the town with my brother and sister and me in order to eat an evening meal, so I felt obliged to decline Christian's friendly invitation. He found this very regrettable, as I did myself, but he did not start begging or complaining. Instead he took hold of his travelling bag, shook me by the hand and said goodbye. As he crossed over the gangway to the shore, he turned once more to wave and smile at me, and I was filled with regret at not having gone with him. At the same moment my mother spoke to me from behind my back; she said that she was sorry that she had not taken a proper farewell of the man who had saved Mary's life. I told her that he was only spending the night in the town and would be returning to the ship the following morning, and I could see that this news pleased her. Encouraged by Mother's reaction, I asked her if she would allow me to accept Christian's invitation to show me the town, and to my surprise she raised no objections. On the contrary, she was unusually generous and said that I was old enough to decide for myself what I wanted to do. Taken by surprise by her sudden change of mood, I thanked her happily and made ready to leave the ship. As I did so Mother held me back for a moment to say that she, Father and my brother and sister had changed their original plan and would now not be going into the town for their evening meal but would be remaining on board instead. At the same time she told me not to be late in returning to the ship; I promised that I would not, and then ran after Christian along the shore, calling his name out loud. He was happy to see me, and once I had explained to him the reason for my sudden appearance and given him my mother's respects, we headed for the town gate, in the company of other passengers who were either, like us, on foot or who had taken a cab. At the gate the gate-keeper asked to see our passports and after Christian and I had shown them to him he allowed us to pass. And so we entered the ancient town of Wesel. The houses had slate roofs, and squeezed among the roofs, towers and gable windows there were several churches. Many of the old stone buildings in the town were decorated with flowers and sculpted friezes.

Evening was falling over the narrow alleys as we walked around, with Christian as my charming guide pointing out the sights and telling me about the town's history. As we crossed the deserted square in front of the town hall, our steps dimly lit by oil lamps, I learned that several illustrious persons had come from Wesel, such as the inventor of the telescope, Hans Lipperhey, and also the founder of the city of New York, Peter Minuit, which I found most remarkable. Christian and I looked at the old town hall and then the mighty cathedral, named after St Willibrord, who Christian told me was an English missionary. We then continued on to the magnificent Berlin Gate, in German called the "Berliner Tor", which is part of the town's defences. When we reached the citadel we suddenly found ourselves confronted with the five officers from the *Stolzenfels*, who were obviously stationed at the fortress of Wesel. Lieutenant Wiessel and his companions made derisive remarks and laughed at Christian's modish apparel, and when we made to pass without responding to their taunts, Wiessel stepped out in front of Christian, blocking his way. He tried to provoke Christian, saying scornfully "Well, have you brought your bodyguard with you", meaning me. Christian stepped aside and we tried to walk away, but Wiessel gripped his arm and hissed at him: "I asked you a question. Why don't you answer me?" Still fully composed, Christian rejoined "Come to the Schill memorial at midnight and I'll give you my answer then. But come alone, without your bodyguard." Thereupon he freed himself from the lieutenant's grip and drew me away from the soldiers, while Wiessel called after us in his resonant voice that he most certainly would appear at the rendez-vous and that Christian should make sure he ordered his coffin.

When I asked Christian why he had made this appointment at the memorial, he answered that he was going to give the lieutenant a warning. I could get no further information out of him, and shortly afterwards we entered an inn called "Zum Schwan" to have our evening meal. We tried to find a place to sit at a long table at which a number of people were already sitting; they were passengers like ourselves, and friendly enough to move closer together so that Christian and I could sit down at the table d'hôte. We put on large serviettes, and then enjoyed our evening meal in pleasant company. The meal consisted of roast duck with apple sauce, and Christian ordered a bottle of the best Rhenish wine. He poured me a glass, and I tasted the delicious drops for the first time. Christian talked about his work as a travelling mineral water representative with a great deal of humour. He had many amusing, and also some tragic, episodes to relate from his travels. About his private life, however, he was less forthcoming, and the only real information I obtained was that he lived sporadically in Bad Ems, and at times with his grandmother in Oberlahnstein, and that he travelled a great deal and was therefore not married. Christian admitted that, despite the large numbers of people he met on his journeys, at bottom he was very lonely, although he comforted himself by saying that at least "a rolling stone gathers no moss". Coming from the mouth of this likeable young man this sounded so infinitely sad that at this moment I was seized by a feeling of great tenderness towards him. I wondered to myself why I had not found him handsome until now, for now his whole laughing face – with his white teeth, cornflower-blue eyes, his prominent chin and suntanned skin with the black stubble of his beard – looked good enough to eat. I concealed the way I was feeling from him, however.

Although he scarcely told me anything about himself Christian wanted to know everything about me, and although I felt shy of letting him look into my life he nonetheless gently lured me into doing so. After we had emptied the first bottle of Hochheimer, Christian ordered a second, and since, as you know dear Gwen, I seldom drink alcohol because it does not agree with me, I was soon rather merry, although I tried my best not to let it show. The wine had also loosened Christian's tongue, and now I did learn something about his private life – namely, that he had been engaged to be married once, but that the relationship had come to an end owing to there being too large differences of character between him and the girl he was betrothed to. After hearing this I thought of telling him about my own misconceived liaison with Henry, but I decided against it, not wanting to compromise myself. Instead I told him about my family and the problems I have been experiencing with my parents. All the frustration caused by their constant arguing, by Mother's malicious nature and coldness, and by Father's compliancy and weakness – frustration which had accumulated in me since I was ten years old – burst out of me. The wine making me heated and talkative, I also expressed my surprise that with my parents, who were completely indifferent to art and culture, I had any artistic ability at all. Christian supposed that there must have been someone further back in my family from whom I had inherited it, and when he said this I suddenly recalled that there had in fact existed such a person, in the form of my great-grandfather Randolph. He was an artistically talented dealer in birds – he gave expression to his talent by using paint and brush to transform the less attractive female birds into better looking, and therefore better selling, males. Christian found this very amusing, but I found it tragic instead, since my great-grandfather had not done it as a joke but as a matter of sheer necessity, since he had a wife and twelve children to support. On listening to this, my travelling companion became serious again, and with great warmth in his voice told me of his parents who, although they had been simple farmers, had been well read. It was a constant sadness to him that they had died at a young age, he said. He had been brought up by his grandmother in the town of Oberlahnstein, where she worked in an inn. From an early age Christian learned to sell drinks, experience which later proved to be of considerable advantage to him in his work as a travelling salesman in mineral water.

Owing to my negative experience of growing up in the house of a merchant, I had actually vowed never to fall in love with a man who, like my father, bought and sold things which other, creative people had made. To my mind a man of commerce is the most unattractive of men, even should he be handsome and possess the best manners. Ever since I was fourteen it has been clear to me that the man of my choice must be someone who makes things of his own; it does not matter in the slightest whether what such a person creates is art or everyday utility objects such as earthenware pots, drinking glasses or saucepans. What is important is that the man makes whatever he creates using the strength of his imagination and his own hands and is not a trader, a seller, even though I have of course always understood that such men are necessary too. This was my definite position, and no argument, however well put, could persuade me otherwise. I was therefore all the more surprised to find that the man in whose company I found myself in a foreign country, and whom I found increasingly agreeable, was precisely one of the breed so detested by me, a salesman. I pushed this realisation aside, by seeking to persuade myself that Christian was not really at heart a salesman, but rather an explorer or scholar, who was only involved in trade in order to guarantee his own subsistence. I found this way of thinking completely legitimate, and at the same time it gave me the reassuring feeling that I did not need to question my conviction as to what type of man is best for me.

5

WHEN ONE is in agreeable company time flies so quickly.
At 10 o'clock, the ringing of bells announced that it was
closing time, and it was time for me to return to the steamer. Christian paid for our food and drink, and we walked
through the sleeping town. The whole place was still and
silent; we saw no candles burning in the windows, and
nobody else at large. We hurried as best we could, but it
was nevertheless too late by the time we reached the town
gate: to my dismay we found it was locked, and the gate-
keeper was nowhere to be seen. When Christian told me
that the gate would not be opened again until the following
morning I was gripped by despair – I had, after all, promised my mother that I would not be late in returning to the
ship. Now, since that was not possible, there was no other

course left open to me than to accompany Christian to his hotel.

For a good 15 minutes we stumbled through the darkened old town and finally came to a large stone building, in which lights were still burning. This was the distinguished-looking hotel the "Dornbusch", in which Christian had taken a room. At the hotel entrance he was given a vigorous welcome by a big, black dog, who jumped all over him and licked him in recognition. The dog did not desist until the hotel manager, an elderly, grey-haired man, shouted a command and the dog immediately went to lie down on an old blanket in the corner. The old man then welcomed Christian and me warmly, and after he had filled in a registration card and the two men, who seemed to know each other well, had exchanged a few more words, the hotel servant showed us to the room where we were to spend the night. I was shocked at the prospect of having to share the room with Christian, and asked him if I might not have a room of my own. He answered that unfortunately the hotel was full and no other room was available. As you know, Gwen, apart from with Henry, my former fiancé, I had never shared a bedroom with a man, far less shared a bed, and I was not at all pleased at being forced to do so now simply because we had gone to the town gate too late. Christian, who could see how I was feeling, comforted me by saying that he would let me have the bed while he himself would sleep on the sofa. At this my anxiety abated somewhat, but when the servant opened the door to a garret room I saw to my dismay that the small room contained no sofa, just a single, narrow bed. The room was clean and orderly, although it was also warm and close. White curtains hung in the window, and the bed linen was white as well. With its thick quilt and pillow the bed looked quite big. Above the head of the bed an etching hung on the wall; it featured a pair of praying hands and was by the artist Albrecht Dürer. A chair stood in front of the sole window, and on the wall there hung a barometer side by side with a thermometer. On the mantlepiece was a vase containing a bouquet of dried flowers. The room was lit by a sorrowful little lamp standing on a writing desk.

The servant held out his hand to demand a tip, and after Christian had given him a couple of coins he wished us a surly *"Gute Nacht"* and left the room, leaving my companion and me standing there with embarrassed expressions on our faces. Christian was the first to recover himself, and saying that the room was very stuffy he walked across to the window and opened it wide to let the cool air in. He then leaned out of the window, looked up into the night sky, and in lyrical tones began praising the beauty of the stars and the cosmos. Christian's enthusiasm conquered my anxiety at being alone with him, and when he said I should join him at the window to see the glory of the night sky for myself, I went across to him and could convince myself of the beauty of the firmament. All at once Christian stepped up onto the chair, and to my horror climbed out onto the roof. However, the roof lay invitingly just beneath our window and was almost flat, so that it was possible to walk on it without there being much danger of slipping and falling to the ground below. Christian held out his hand and entreated me to step out onto the roof and join him, so that I could gain a better view of the stars. At first I refused to comply with his request, which in my eyes seemed rather foolhardy, but at length, worn down by his powers of persuasion, I yielded. Christian took me by the hand and showed me a place where I could lay on my back. I did as he said, and he lay down beside me, and we lay there gazing up at the star-studded firmament which arched above us like a black velvet blanket strewn with millions of sparkling diamonds. Christian pointed to a constellation directly above us and said: "Can you see those stars there? That's the Great Bear and the Little Bear, and there in the north, that's Cassiopeia".

He then pointed out another constellation, next to Cassiopeia, and said that it was Andromeda. On hearing the name Andromeda I suddenly remembered the story from Greek mythology, and told Christian that Andromeda was a princess who was to be sacrificed to a sea-monster. He asked me if the princess had fallen victim to the monster, and I said that she was rescued by Pegasus at the very last minute. Thereupon Christian once more pointed up into the night sky and said that Pegasus, too, could be seen up there. He explained to me that the stars are immensely far apart, with the distances between them being measured in millions of miles. If the distance between the earth and the sun were one inch, he explained, then the next nearest star would be 40 miles away. And that is why, he said, continuing his lesson, stars look like small dots of light, and why they are always seen to be in the same position in relation to one another, which, Christian said emphatically, is a fact of fundamental importance.

"You seem to know a lot about astronomy", I observed, and he replied that he had been interested in the subject ever since he was six years old. He told me that in the evenings, when it was dark and the sky was clear, he would go outside, a map of the heavens in his hand, and look up at the stars, memorising the constellations. I interjected that I was unsure of what the difference was between astrology and astronomy; Christian replied that the two disciplines were as different from each other as chalk and cheese. He explained to me that astronomy is the study of the heavens, and is above all an exact science, whereas astrology is no more than a medieval superstition, a harmless pastime as long as it is viewed as a drawing-room entertainment. When I asked him why he had not become an astronomer when he knew so much about it, he replied that he had indeed wanted to, but that his family had not had enough money for him to be able to pursue an education in the science. I thought this was a shame, since I was convinced that he would have made an excellent astronomer.

A moment's silence arose on the roof, and then I said, turning to Christian: "You'll never guess what I wanted to be when I was a child". He guessed painter, in response to which I shook my head and said "a magician". This sounded so silly to my ears that I blushed, although Christian, who gave me a look of surprise, probably couldn't see this in the gloom on the roof.

"I can just picture you as a magician, Miss Dubb", he said with a smile, and before I could reply he went on: "In fact, I think you've cast a spell on me." While saying this he leant over me to kiss me, but I pushed him away, disappointed by his over-hasty, and what is more unoriginal, approach. I gave Christian to understand that just because we were alone in the dark, that did not automatically mean that he could take liberties with me. I warned him not to make any further such attempt, which he promised, filled with remorse and contrition. I then clambered to my feet, and on uncertain legs walked over to the window and climbed back into the room. A moment later Christian also came back inside, and declared: "I don't know why I acted like that, that's not what I'm usually like." He then asked me, with an innocent look, "Can you forgive me, Miss Idilia?"

I said that I forgave him, although I really felt that I

should not forgive him so easily, but should rather let him suffer for a while longer. However, Christian's likeable nature weakened my resolve and I soon forgot the moral indignation which in truth I had only half-heartedly felt at his unseemly behaviour. I was just about to ask him how he envisaged that we should sleep in the small room with its single bed, when he pulled his pocket watch out and, looking at it, found that it was time for him to go to his rendez-vous with the Prussian lieutenant at the Schill statue. I had forgotten all about this, and immediately started trying to convince Christian of the incredible foolishness of risking his health, perhaps even his life, for the sake of a misconceived idea of honour and exaggerated pride. For his part, Christian refused to listen to me. He said he was determined to pay the lieutenant back once and for all, which made me lose my patience with him yet again. However, he merely shrugged his shoulders, and advised me to go to sleep and not stay up on his account. I retorted in a scornful tone that, bearing in mind the ridiculous conduct he was preparing, I would certainly not sit up and wait for him. That was what I said, but when he had left the bedroom and I had heard his footsteps die away on the stairs, I knew that I would not be able to close my eyes until he had returned to me safe and sound.

In order to help the time pass more quickly, I sat down at the secretaire in the hotel room and wrote my diary.

Monday, 9th June 1851

Shortly after 2 am I heard footsteps on the stairs. A moment later the door was opened from the outside, and to my alarm I saw Christian, his face covered in blood and his clothes all torn, standing unsteadily in the doorway. I dropped my pencil and ran over to him. "What in heaven's name has happened?" I asked him, as I helped him to the bed and pulled back the quilt so that he could lie down comfortably.

"The damned lieutenant didn't come alone. He had his chums with him", Christian answered, his face distorted from pain. "Luckily I had the landlord's dog with me, otherwise it might have turned out much worse", he added, as he lay down on his back.

My first impulse was to remind Christian that I had warned him not to go to the rendez-vous with the lieutenant, but I held my tongue out of consideration for the wretched condition in which he found himself. I took out a large handkerchief from my dress, wet it with water from a porcelain jug standing on the washstand, and washed the blood from Christian's face. While I was tending him thus I asked him all about what had taken place, and learned that the lieutenant and his companions had planned to put an end to him with their swords. However, the hotel-keeper's dog, which Christian had taken with him just in case, was able to thwart their plan: he had hurled himself at Christian's assailants, bitten them so severely that they were put out of action, and finally put to flight. In the course of the battle the dog had itself incurred a few sword blows, but these were only superficial wounds and were not serious. Christian told me that the landlord had already patched up the dog's injuries, and shortly afterwards I too had stopped the bleeding from my German companion's face and hands. After that I removed his tattered blue tail coat, and having removed my outer clothes I lay down on the bed in my petticoat next to Christian, who looked astonished as I did so. I was certain that in his condition he was scarcely likely to get sufficiently carried away to attempt any further impropriety, and that it was therefore perfectly safe to lie down in the same bed as him; moreover, he had given me his word that he would behave correctly and not for a minute did I doubt that he would keep his promise. We talked for a little while about the events of the day, and soon fell asleep, lying side by side like a couple who were well used to sleeping in the same bed.

I dreamt that I was on the steamer; I saw Christian kissing me – he was sitting in his armchair on the foredeck, and was holding me captive, tied up in his fishing line. Suddenly I heard a bang, and when I looked up I saw my mother standing on the bridge holding a shotgun, smoke coming out of its muzzle. I was woken by the bang, and immediately understood that it was the signal shot from the *Stolzenfels*, and that Christian and I had overslept. Christian was already up, and when he saw that I was awake he urged me to get up straight away so that we would not miss our ship, which was timetabled to leave at 7 am. I did not need to be told twice, and shortly afterwards the two of us, untidily dressed and with uncombed hair, stormed downstairs to the ground floor. Nobody else in the hotel was up, and we had to spend some time looking for the hotel keeper. Christian finally found him in the backyard, and once he had paid for our room, we rushed out of the hotel.

The streets of the little town were still empty and silent. The only signs of life were one or two nightingales competing with each other, and the splashing of a fountain. When we reached the town gate we found it still locked. The gate-keeper came out, rubbing the sleep from his eyes, and wished us "Guten Morgen". As he opened the gate for us —I was astonished all over again by the splendour of the Rhine landscape revealed in the rising sun: the smooth lines of the mountains, the wide mirror-like expanse of the river, and the transparent veils of mist drifting over the water.

We ran down to the shore, and were dismayed to see the *Stolzenfels* chugging upstream, with black smoke billowing from its funnel. I looked around, in the hope of discovering that my parents and brother and sister were not on board the steamer, but had stayed behind on the shore to wait for me and a later boat. However, they were nowhere to be seen, and I assumed that my mother, indignant at my failing to appear in time, had forced the rest of my family to stay on board and continue the journey without me. I felt very disappointed at being punished by her in this way, and thought that what a fellow passenger on the ship had said about Mother had been true, namely that she was a woman with the blood of a viper, and that was why she was so malicious. Before I could brood any longer on that theme, however, Christian grabbed me by the arm and indicated that I should follow him: we ran side by side along the shore towards a pontoon bridge over the river, while the *Stolzenfels* was making for the same bridge at full steam. Christian was hoping to be able to get the steamer to stop at the bridge, but as we approached it, quite out of breath, we saw that the bridge keeper had opened it and that the steamer was just on its way through at unreduced speed. We shouted and waved our arms in the attempt to get the captain and his crew to stop, but they either could not hear us, or else chose not to hear us, for the great paddles of the *Stolzenfels* did not slow in the slightest as the ship continued its way upstream, leaving Christian and me standing on the pontoon bridge, exhausted and disappointed. When the bridge keeper had closed the middle section of the bridge again, Christian decided that we should return to Wesel and take the other steamer which was standing at its moorings with smoke rising from its funnel. Having undertaken an intensive jog back to the town we made our way to the "Comptoir", a small cabin serving as a ticket office, to buy tickets. There was already a considerable crowd of people jostling and pushing to reach the cashiers. Christian and I worked our way through the turmoil to the counter and bought two tickets to Düsseldorf, where we hoped to be able to catch up with the *Stolzenfels* again and continue on to Coblenz together with my family.

At long last we were allowed over a narrow, enclosed gangway onto the passenger paddle-steamer the *König*. A bell rang to announce our departure, the engines shuddered into life, and shortly afterwards the ship cast off, shaking and groaning. As the paddle-wheels whipped the water, and the steamer steered through the narrow channel formed by a silted-up arm of the Rhine and began to leave Wesel behind, we looked around us in despair, for every single place where it would have been agreeable to sit was already occupied. The only empty spaces we could see were next to the burning hot funnel, and since the smoke from a ship's funnel leaves unsuspecting passengers who sit too close dusted with soot, we had no desire to sit there. To move around the vessel we had to fight our way through the throngs of men, women and children who were hectically trying to extract their travelling effects from a mountain of bags and packages.

Towards the bows Christian and I finally managed to locate a place, although only on the floor, since on the forecastle as elsewhere on the ship every chair and bench was occupied. We made ourselves as comfortable as was possible, and observed the busy goings-on on board and the beautiful countryside on view on both sides of the ship. We ordered breakfast from a steward, consisting of broth, eggs, cheese and black bread, to accompany which we drank hot tea. As we ate, Christian told me of the chequered history of the Rhine valley: of the Celts, who were the first people to settle here; of the Romans, who came later and cultivated the region; and of the English missionaries who converted the Rhenish heathens to Christianity. I heard a great deal about robber barons, who wreaked their mischief along the Rhine in the middle ages, and I learned that most of the castles of the region do not stem from those times, but are in fact much younger than that. I listened to Christian with interest, and asked questions from time to time which he patiently tried to answer. The time passed very quickly, and as the hour approached 10 am we reached the town of Duisburg, where the ship halted briefly to set down some passengers and take aboard some new ones. Christian availed himself of this opportunity to go and talk to the captain of our ship, who told him that in Düsseldorf, the next stopping point on our journey, it should be possible for us to regain the *Stolzenfels*, since at 12.15, the timetabled arrival time of the *König*, the *Stolzenfels* would still be lying at its moorings in that port.

While looking forward to arriving soon in Düsseldorf, Christian and I walked back and forth around the ship, watching our fellow passengers or enjoying the wonderful Rhineland scenery which, with its infinite wealth of meadows and pastures, small towns and villages, low lands and mountains, made me feel as if an immense monumental painting was being unfolded before us. When we had had enough of looking at the countryside, my companion and I lay down on our backs on the deck, gazed up into the cloudless blue of the sky and engaged in philosophical conversation. Christian compared our journey on a steamship along the Rhine with the course of the Earth through the universe, at the end of which we would find ourselves confronted by an unknown destiny. For my part I rather saw our journey as a good opportunity for gaining experience and impressions which could be of value in later life.

Fatigued by these cogitations I soon fell asleep; however, the hard deck under me was too uncomfortable to allow of lengthy slumber, and after a while I woke up again. I discovered that Christian was no longer lying beside me; looking around I saw him standing on the bridge next to the captain, pointing with an outstretched arm in a southerly direction. When I looked in the direction he was indicating I perceived what seemed to be a large town, and the steam-ship the *Stolzenfels* moving away from the town and making for the middle of the river. I looked at my pocket watch, and saw that the hour was 12.35, and when Christian came back over to me a moment later he told me that our steamer, the *König*, was running late and had missed the *Stolzenfels*. However, Christian continued, the German captain had promised that, in return for a couple of packets of Dutch tobacco, he would catch up with our ship and set us down on it. This sounded uncommonly hazardous to my ears, and indeed so it proved to be. The captain, driven by the desire to fulfil his promise to Christian and earn his reward, took up the pursuit of the *Stolzenfels*. The sailors brought up big lumps of coal which the stoker fed into the puffing and hissing steam engine. I feared that at any moment the engine would explode, but Christian, attempting to calm my anxiety, said that the infernal machine was not at all dangerous. However, I felt unable to place complete trust in his words, so I stood at a distance, watching uneasily as the engine swallowed more and more coal; the more the stoker fed into the machine, the more steam it produced, and the more steam there was in the boiler, the faster the paddle-wheels turned. The distance between us and the *Stolzenfels* grew ever shorter, but since the captain of that vessel made no sign of slowing down it soon seemed that we were engaged in an out-and-out race between the Dutch and the German ship. Finally, when the *König* had caught up with the *Stolzenfels* and the two steamers were side by side, Christian took me by the hand, wanting to leap over onto the other ship with me, but I was frightened lest I should fall between the two hulls into the water, and refused to jump. When the captain of the *König* then yelled to us from the bridge to get a move on and jump, since he could not hold his ship in that position any longer, Christian took his cue: he shouted to the passengers at the rail of the *Stolzenfels* to stand back, threw his travelling bag over onto the other ship, and then, without hesitation, leapt after it himself. Thereupon he stood at the rail with his arms stretched out towards me, exhorting me to jump over to him, but I was unable to overcome my fear, not even when my brother and sister appeared beside Christian and called to me to dare to leap. I stood there as if paralysed, and the longer I hesitated, the greater became the gap between the two steamers.

When Christian realised that the gap had become so wide that it was now impossible for me to jump, he gathered all his strength and jumped back to me on the *König*, landing with a fall on the deck, although he was able directly afterwards to regain his feet. Christian's brave leap, which must certainly have been of a good three metres, drew applause from the other passengers, although my brother and sister, seeing our separation thus prolonged, looked far from happy. I had scarcely shouted out to them: "Don't worry, we'll soon be together again" when the *König* reduced speed, swung round in a wide arc, and began steaming downstream towards Düsseldorf, while the *Stolzenfels* continued pounding up-river towards its next destination, Cologne.

Christian was uninjured after his daring leap, but he was angry that what he called my "exaggerated fearfulness" had prevented us from regaining the *Stolzenfels*. The captain of the *König* also saw in this a cause for indignation, since he had pursued the other steamer, thereby "making a mess" of the timetable of his Düsseldorf steamship company "for no reason at all". Indeed, even the other passengers, who would have liked to see us succeed in transferring to the other ship in mid-river, now started giving me contemptuous looks and comments; the result was that I felt that every other person on board viewed me as an outcast.

I could see that Christian suffered from this, but since he said nothing about forgiving me for my lack of courage I fixed a closed and chilly expression on my face and let him feel how wretched I found his behaviour. I was not, however, able to ignore him for long, for upon our arrival in Düsseldorf he shocked me with the bad news that all his money was in the bag he had thrown onto the *Stolzenfels*, which meant that he now had no money to buy tickets to Cologne, which was where we wanted to regain that ship. I did not have any money either, and when Christian made a desperate appeal to the captain of the *König* to take us there free of charge he refused, on the grounds that we had already had one opportunity to get back on board our original ship, but had not taken advantage of it. No amount of begging and pleading by Christian could persuade the captain to change his mind, and thus we found ourselves with no choice but to disembark from his boat and make our way out of Düsseldorf on foot.

6

AFTER LEAVING the town behind us we walked southwards along a dusty, hole-ridden country road. We tried to induce passing travellers in their carriages and diligences to stop and let us travel with them to Cologne, but not a single conveyance halted. Seeing our predicament, I became bad-tempered, and gave Christian to understand that he should leave me alone and not follow me, since I was extremely annoyed at the disagreeable turn the journey had taken and was of the opinion that it was solely thanks to Christian's ludicrous dispute with the lieutenant in Wesel that I now found myself, separated from my family and without any money, having to find my way in a strange country. The more I mused on this the more infuriated I became, and I stormed along the road with quick strides and my mouth pressed closed. My travelling companion did not, however, pay any heed to my demand and followed after me, although he had some difficulty in keeping up with the rapid speed at which I was walking. Soon he was some twenty-five yards behind me, and thereafter we maintained this distance between us. From time to time a carriage came by, but however much we waved and shouted, none of the drivers stopped to take us on our way southwards.

The weather was glorious, and it was very hot. Since I had not had anything to eat or drink for a long time I suddenly felt weak and had to sit down to rest on a large rock at the side of the road. A minute or two later Christian came up to me, and sat down beside me. He said he understood that I was angry with him for causing us to miss the steamer, but promised to see to it that we were soon on board a ship and heading south. He offered me some water from one of his earthenware jars, and as provender gave me a piece of sausage, which I accepted only with reluctance and ate out of my hand. This slight repast did not soften my mood towards Christian; instead I told him crossly that the water was warm and the sausage too salty, and at this he lost his patience and said that if I did not find his food or his presence agreeable then I should go somewhere else. I immediately complied with his wish, jumping to my feet and setting off again, while Christian remained sitting, watching me walk away and shaking his head.

Shortly afterwards a trap being drawn by a single horse halted beside me, and a middle-aged man dressed in black offered me a ride. Tempted by the prospect of being reunited with my family soon, and not being obliged to struggle my way through foreign parts at the side of the swanking Christian, I forgot the caution I usually observe when addressed by men I do not know, and climbed up onto the trap and sat down next to the driver. Being now able to examine him more closely, I discovered that he did not look very trustworthy, but it was already too late to jump down from the vehicle. I heard Christian shouting to me from behind not to accept the man's offer of a ride just as the driver gave a crack of his whip to urge his horse to a trot and the trap rolled off in a cloud of dust.

The man spoke broken English, and as we drove along we talked about the heat, which by now was surely in advance of 70 degrees. Thereafter he complained of being lonely since his wife had died, and complimented me on my appearance. After we had been driving for about ten minutes he turned into a wood, and halted his horse. He then threw himself upon me, trying to kiss me and tear off my dress. Before he could fulfil his intention, however, Christian suddenly appeared and hurled himself at my aggressor, who had taken down his breeches so that they hung around his knees. A wild fight ensued, the result of which was that Christian and I ended up pushing the trap-owner out of the carriage. Christian grabbed the reins, made a clicking noise with his mouth, and steered the trap out of the wood, leaving its defeated owner behind us in the grass, roaring with pain and rage.

When we were back on the main road I expressed my surprise that Christian had been so quick in turning up to intervene in my defence; he replied that the sight of the driver of the trap had given him a bad feeling in his stomach, and so he had run after us, determined to save me from the man. I smiled at Christian and said that I was very lucky that he had, since had it not been for his courageous intervention I would certainly have been made to suffer badly. I thanked him for the bravery he had shown on my account, and begged his pardon for having been so obstinate towards him before. Christian waved my remarks aside, however, saying that he understood that I was upset at having missed the steamer to Cologne, and renewing his promise to bring me back together with my family before long. How exactly he intended to achieve that objective remained a mystery to me, bearing in mind that the *Stolzenfels* had disappeared from view a long time since, and we could only make slow progress in the trap along the sandy, stony, rutted and puddle-strewn road. Nevertheless, Christian's optimism, humour and good temper, which had remained intact through all the hardships and nuisances we had encountered, appealed to me and the longer the cross-country journey which circumstances had obliged us to take progressed, the more I came to value my German companion.

Christian thought that we had good hopes of catching up with the *Stolzenfels* in the town of Cologne, which was still several miles distant. In his endeavour to reach the town in time he drove the horse to its limits, so that we bowled along up hill and down dale. Our wild drive took us at places along the river bank, as well as through much attractive countryside and many pretty villages. It is well-nigh impossible to describe the diversity and splendour of all the things which passed before our eyes in rapid succession. Just when one believed that one had seen the most beautiful prospect, another, still more captivating scene presented itself, in which however we had no time to take delight since we had our minds set on regaining our steamship without having to spend any further days on the dusty, rutted road. Moreover, however well our horse was drawing us, at the speed with which we were going we had to reckon on its soon becoming exhausted; in other words, it would not be able to take us all the way to our final destination, Coblenz, which was still a couple of hundred miles away.

Unfortunately, when we had traversed approximately half the distance to Cologne our trap sustained a broken wheel, when Christian drove too quickly over a large stone in the road. In fact, the trap was close to turning over, and it was only thanks to his great skill as a coachman that we escaped unscathed. The accident having occurred a good distance short of the next village, and it being impossible for us to repair the broken wheel, we had no other choice but to unhitch the black horse and leave the trap by the side of the road. Christian swung himself up onto the saddle-less horse, helped me up and off we rode, me clinging anxiously to Christian's back.

It was not as pleasant riding as I had imagined but it was no less hard and uncomfortable than it had been sitting in the speeding trap. And in fact, after a short while I became used to this means of locomotion. I even found myself enjoying it, holding on tight against Christian's broad back, with the clip-clopping of the horse's hooves in my ears and the regular see-sawing rhythm with which I was being carried along – up and down, up and down. I closed my eyes, and smiled at the thought of what you, Gwen, would have said at the sight of your otherwise so reserved friend Idilia, sitting behind a good-looking young man on a black horse, like the heroine in a romantic novel, riding towards an imaginary destination beyond the hazy horizon. You would surely not have recognised me, and neither would my parents or brother and sister, since you all know me as the Idilia who is always orderly and well-behaved, but also rather boring; the Idilia who never acts out of character or allows herself to get carried away and be spontaneous or do anything wildly unpredictable. Being sweet and gentle and never any trouble was always part of my nature, as was the friendly and obedient disposition which from an early age enabled me to save my strength and survive in a hostile world such as school. As you yourself know, Gwen, I was always top of the class at school, never the second-best or third-best, and so everyone who knew me assumed that later in life, when I was an adult, I would be just as clever and dutiful. However, despite all that, for seventeen years I have felt myself to be a loser, because I felt I was left on my own, and that paralysed me. But now here I was: I had turned my back on Henry, joined my family on this journey to Germany against my Mother's wishes, and was now galloping across the country with a man I hardly knew – and I was enjoying the feeling of no longer being the nice, boring Idilia who believed she could only live in accordance with a predetermined plan. It was very exciting for me not to know for once what the next minute, the next hour, the next week would bring. Clearly, I could not live in such a way indefinitely; I knew that in time I could expect the old, orderly Idilia to reveal herself again and the fun to end. Until then, however, I felt determined to enjoy my newly won freedom to the full, and let myself be carried along by a stream of feelings that were new to me, feelings aroused by my physical closeness to Christian, the beauty of nature on view all around me, and the reassuring knowledge that I was a long, long way away from my mother.

From time to time Christian reined our sweat-covered horse to a halt so that we could stretch our legs and have a drink of water from a stream or well. Thus refreshed, we resumed our ride through the Rhine valley, drawing ever closer to our destination, Cologne. After a time our hard-working mount lost a shoe, however, which meant that our speed diminished, since we had to dismount at ever more frequent intervals and walk along beside the limping animal in order not to expose it to suffering. We came to a small village, where Christian tried to persuade a big, burly blacksmith to shoe our horse free of charge. The blacksmith refused, but then changed his mind when his eyes fell on me, and declared that he would help us if, as payment, he could have a kiss from me. Since I was afraid that we might not reach Cologne in time and would therefore miss our steamer again, I forgot for a moment the repugnance the blacksmith inspired in me, covered head to foot as he was in soot and dirt, and gave him a peck on the cheek. Not content at that, he drew me towards him and gave me a big kiss right on the lips. I was outraged, tore myself out of his grasp and slapped him hard in the face. This did not seem to bother the smith, though, who responded by laughing and giving me a teasing pinch on the cheek. He then set about shoeing our horse, humming happily to himself. I felt like nothing more than giving the blacksmith a kick in his broad behind, and could see by the look on Christian's face that he was entertaining similar thoughts. For understandable reasons, however, we restrained ourselves. Christian pointed out that there was a patch of soot on my cheek where the blacksmith had pinched it, and when I was unable to remove it he carefully cleaned my face with his handkerchief. When the smith had finally finished shoeing the horse and handed it back to us my ill-humour at his unruly behaviour had had time to subside, and as he helped me to mount and wished me a "pleasant journey" I even thanked him with a slight smile. Christian, on the other hand, was still angry at the lack of respect the smith had shown, and rode off without any parting greeting, and without thanking the smith for his assistance.

With the new shoe on its hoof our horse soon rediscovered his old form, and despite the fact that he had already carried Christian and me a great distance on his back, he surprised us by showing no signs of exhaustion, or even of tiredness.

As we rode along I tried to converse with Christian, but since whatever I said only elicited a monosyllabic "yes" or "no" I soon gave up. He appeared to be brooding about something, and I assumed it was the kiss stolen by the blacksmith that was the cause of his bad temper and disinclination to talk. When I asked him if this was the case, after an initial denial Christian finally admitted that he was still feeling very upset at the blacksmith's insolence. I found this very touching, and said, with some amusement, that he surely understood that he had no need to be jealous of that boorish, ugly man. Hereupon my companion denied that he was jealous – although his voice, his attitude and his behaviour betrayed that this was exactly how he was feeling. I could not hold his feelings against him, Gwen, since as you are aware I am not proof against jealousy myself. Henry, my former fiancé, knows all about how to inflict this torment – his constant affairs often left me a prey to it. I thought of the faithless Henry while I rode through the beautiful Rhineland countryside, sitting behind Christian on our black horse, and came to the conclusion that Henry's unfaithfulness was my very good fortune, since without it I would never have met Christian or tasted this new, completely different life.

I was roused from these musings when we once more came to a village well, at which both mount and riders drank eagerly of the cool water. As we rode on we began to leave the flat lands of the Lower Rhineland behind us, and drew ever nearer to Cologne.

We reached our destination shortly after sunset, arriving at a landing stage in Cologne where we encountered an animated crowd of people waiting to depart. They streamed up the gangways in droves, and one over-filled ship after another cast off. However, just as we were making to go aboard the *Stolzenfels* Christian discovered to his dismay that his ticket had disappeared; he supposed that he had lost it in the course of his set-to with the owner of the trap. Christian explained his situation to the conductor, who nevertheless refused to allow him on board unless he purchased a new ticket. This of course he was unable to do, since he had no money about his person, and as I too was without money but in possession of my ticket, I decided to go on board and ask my parents to give Christian the money for a new ticket. He had, after all, saved my sister's life, and helped me to get back to the ship, so to my mind a ticket for the steamer was the least they could do to pay him back for all his selflessness. Christian, however, wanted to pay for his ticket himself, and asked me to fetch him his travelling bag, in which he had his money.

I told Christian to wait for me and hurried aboard to look for his bag and my parents. Being unable to locate the bag anywhere I kept a lookout for my parents, and soon bumped into my father. He gave me a dumbfounded look, and said, in astonishment, "Where've you come from, Idilia?" I answered that I could tell him all about it later, but that first I needed money for a ticket to Coblenz. Believing that I had lost my own ticket Father immediately pulled some coins from his pocket and pressed them into my hand. I ran back to the gangway, but just as I reached it I saw two crew members pulling it onto the ship, which had slowly started moving away from the shore. And there I saw Christian, his hair matted with perspiration and with an expression of confusion on his dust-covered face. He was standing beside the horse, and he looked so lonely and abandoned that I at once decided to rejoin him. I pushed a couple of the passengers at the rail to one side, gathered all my strength and took a giant leap onto the shore. On landing I fell heavily to the ground. Christian hurried over to me and enquired in a worried tone whether I had accomplished my daring leap without injury. I was indeed most surprised to find that I had, since the distance from the ship to the landing stage must certainly have been something in the order of three yards; however, my spontaneous desire to stay with Christian had somehow given me supernatural strength and enabled me to jump safely over to the quayside. I showed him the money which my father had given me, and he thanked me, clearly moved, for my help and for my decision not to stay on the steamer as long as he was not on it. As we sat watching the *Stolzenfels* back out into the middle of the river and then resume its upstream course with black smoke churning out of the funnel, Christian and I discussed how we could go about accomplishing the long journey to Coblenz which lay ahead of us with the small amount of money at our disposal. Finding ourselves unable to arrive at any answer, we resolved that we would begin by washing off the dust we had accumulated during our cross-country trek.

A few minutes later we stood at a fountain in the town, cleaning our hands and faces, when Christian suddenly hit upon the idea of selling the horse and using the money to buy a ticket to travel with the next ship. He had no scruples about doing this, he said, since the owner of the horse had forfeited his right to the animal by attacking me. I was of a mind with Christian and thought it was an excellent idea, especially as I was heartily tired of being shaken through and through on the beast's back.

Since our long journey had left us hungry and thirsty, and the hour being too late for us to sell our horse, we walked through the twilit town looking for an inn where we might eat our first real meal of the day. In Cologne there are a great many beer and coffee gardens for the ordinary people, and for the "better classes", or the "beautiful people" as the well-to-do are known in Germany, there are arbours, round places surrounded by screens of bushes so that the diners could eat without every passer-by being able to see what they had on their plates. Christian, who had tied up our horse at one of these arbours close to the city's colossal cathedral, decided on the spot that we belonged to the class of "beautiful people", despite the fact that we did not have very much money and did not at that moment look particularly beautiful. Christian was no longer wearing a tail coat; he was wearing a waistcoat and a white shirt which had long since taken on a grey colour from all the dust to which we had been exposed on our journey. Christian's boots, like my shoes, were not in a polished condition, and my dress, like his trousers, bore visible signs of having suffered from the adventures we had undergone. A quick look in my pocket mirror made me shudder, since I saw that my face was stained with perspiration, and that my hair was full of dust which made it look grey instead of strawberry blonde. Not only that, in addition there was hardly anything left of what had once been a handsome hairstyle. I quickly put the mirror away in order to avoid becoming downhearted; it is only fairly recently that I have begun to be able to accept my appearance and like myself, and I had no wish to fall back into my old self-despisal.

Christian and I stepped into an arbour which was filled with well-dressed people who watched us with curiosity while we sought an unoccupied table. After we had sat down I saw them whispering comments behind their hands regarding our presence there. They made no effort to conceal the fact that they were staring at us, so I asked Christian, raising my voice so that they would be able to hear me, if it was the custom in Germany to gape insolently at people one does not know. He answered ashamedly that it is not customary, and told me not to take any notice of all the people there, since they probably could not speak any English and were therefore not in a position to understand what I said. I followed his advice and paid no more heed to the people around us, and soon they in their turn seemed to lose their interest in us. A courteous waiter appeared, from whom Christian ordered a bottle of Rhenish wine and a genuine German supper, consisting of liver dumplings and sauerkraut. The meal left us so we were fit to burst.

An hour later I paid for our wine and food with my father's money and we left the restaurant, well replete but with almost no money left at all. Christian untied the horse from the arbour and we walked around the town for a while, it being a city I had not previously visited. Evening fell over the narrow alleys, and we set off in search of a simple hotel, even though we did not have enough money to pay for a room for the night. Christian hoped that he would be able to sell the horse the following morning, and believed that the proceeds of the sale would cover the cost of a hotel room as well as two steam-ship tickets. Before long we found a small hotel in which lights were still burning, and after he had asked the hotel-keeper – an unbelievably fat, red-haired woman aged about forty – and made sure that there indeed was a room available for the night, Christian tied up our horse in the stable in the backyard. We then dealt with the formalities, were given a lighted candle in a candlestick by the red-haired hotel-keeper along with a wrought iron key, and climbed the steep stairs to the third floor. The room, and the bed, in which we were to spend the night were even smaller than our accommodation of the previous night in Wesel. The window, too, was very much smaller in our Cologne room, and to Christian's disappointment did not allow us to climb out onto the roof to observe the stars in the night sky. Despite the strenuous journey we had made neither of us was at all tired, so we sat on the bed and played a simple game of cards, in order to pass the time. The game soon degenerated into general tomfoolery between the two of us; we suddenly found ourselves very close to each other, and when Christian almost tried to kiss me I decided it was time for us to end the game. I told Christian that I had something I had to do, and took out my diary and some writing paper.

In order to occupy himself, Christian tried, in vain, to wind up an old wall-clock which hung, its pointers motionless, on the wall of the hotel room; while he did so he went on at great length about how long one single minute could seem to him sometimes. To demonstrate to me what he meant, he put the big hand of his pocket watch at twelve and started counting the seconds. At the end of sixty seconds I had to agree that a minute seemed endlessly long to me, too. After this experiment I commenced writing a farewell letter to Henry; I had long intended to send him such a letter, but had never found the occasion to get it done. When Christian discovered that I was writing to another man he fell completely silent, and looked dejected. He said he needed to go out and take the air, saying that it was very close in our room. Before I could do anything to prevent him he went out through the door and hurried noisily down the stairs. I resolved not to let his behaviour bother me, and by the light of the candle I finished my letter to Henry and then opened my diary and summarised the events of this Monday.

At about 10pm I heard a night watch blowing his horn to announce that it was closing time, but still Christian did not return to me in our room. The hour progressed to 11, and then to midnight, and I gradually started to worry that he should remain absent for so long.

Tuesday, 10th June 1851
Why, oh why, my dear Gwen, do I always have to be caused so much trouble by men? No sooner have I found someone who is not only kind and intelligent but in addition thereto is also attractive in appearance, than the positive picture I have been able to form of him is clouded by some other, less pleasant characteristic. In Christian's case it is his jealousy, which showed itself soon after we had first made each other's acquaintance, and announces its presence in the form of a dejected expression, wordlessness and then flight. It is a pity, because I otherwise find him very likeable, and was even on the verge of falling a little in love with him – but this bad behaviour, running away in the middle of the night and leaving me, in a state of anxiety in a strange town, to wait for him, led to the warm feelings I had felt for him once more becoming cool.

Half an hour after midnight, at which hour I was still sitting on the bed writing in my diary, I heard someone crashing up the stairs; shortly afterwards the door was opened from the outside and in came Christian. He was drunk, and was holding a wine-bottle in his hand. I asked him, in a tone filled with reproach, where he had been, but he did not answer, returning my question with one of his own: he asked in a slurred voice if my friend Henry in England could do such good tricks as he could. Thereupon he raised the bottle of wine to his lips and emptied it in a single draught. He then belched loudly and let the bottle fall to the floor, stood there swaying for a moment, and then fell headlong, landing beside me on the bed. He mumbled "We really must catch the steamer" and then fell instantly asleep. He started snoring, and my initial indignation at his inebriated condition soon gave way to a feeling of sympathy with him when I realised that it was because my letter had made him unhappy that he had sought solace in drink. I lay my diary aside, and then eased a pillow under Christian's head. I extinguished the candle, and after lying awake thinking for quite some while in the dark of the night, and recalling with a smile the improbable adventures of that day, at length I too fell asleep.

7

IT WAS A very early hour – indeed, scarcely 4 am – and the cockerels were just starting to crow when Christian woke me and told me to get up without delay. I was still half asleep and could only form a hazy idea of where I was. When Christian prodded me again and repeated his instruction I asked him sleepily why he was in such a hurry; he told me that the previous evening, in a game of cards at an inn, he had staked our horse and lost, so that consequently we had no money to pay for our hotel room. I was immediately wide awake and stared at Christian thunderstruck, who explained to me ashamedly that we had no alternative but to take to our heels before the landlady woke up. I had a good mind to give him a proper dressing down for his stupidity, but I thought better of it since nothing could undo what had happened, and besides, he assured me in a manner I believed that he had only started playing cards in an attempt to win the money we needed for the rest of our journey. Unfortunately the other players were more skilful than he and so he had ended up losing our black horse. I decided not to dwell on this mishap, and not to reproach him for the loss; instead I rapidly gathered together my belongings and we crept out of the hotel like two thieves, without being observed by anyone. Once we were outdoors we ran as fast as we could through the quiet, deserted alleys and streets towards the city gate, casting occasional anxious glances over our shoulders to make sure that we were not being pursued by the landlady or the police. We heard the melodious pealing of church bells ringing for morning worship, and the rising sun turned the roofs of the houses to shimmering gold. When we reached the city gate the surly gate-keeper opened it to let us out, and we hastened away from the ancient town of Cologne. A fresh, cool morning wind blew into our faces as we walked along the left bank of the Rhine on a country road, the surface of which was made of unhewn stone. Our next destination was the town of Bonn, which lay 22 miles ahead of us. And from there we hoped that there we would be able to find a steam-ship or diligence with which we could travel free of charge to Coblenz.

In the course of our march southwards we had ample

opportunity to enoy the beautiful countryside, which enabled us to forget the long distance we had to traverse. Outside Cologne extended a plain which ended against a chain of mountains. Light veils of mist lay picturesquely over the noble river with its greenish water. At one point there was an opening in the mist and we could see across to the opposite bank, along which there stood occasional cottages. A couple of fishermen rowed past, singing their morning song at the top of their lungs. Inspired by all these pictures, I made some landscape sketches.

Before very long the mist rose and the sun started shining down on us. Christian and I strolled on, and from time to time we sat down on the river bank and the sun warmed us so much that we decided to refresh ourselves by bathing. At a seemly distance from each other we undressed in the reeds until we were in our underclothes, and then splashed around for a while in the cool water. Thus refreshed, we dressed ourselves again and resumed our southward march along the country road.

The amount of traffic along the road began to increase, and more and more frequently we saw gigs and diligences coming towards us from the direction of Bonn, or were overtaken by conveyances coming from Cologne. We gestured and called to these latter in the hope that someone would stop and allow us to travel with them, but covered with dust and perspiration as we were, we must have presented such an off-putting sight that nobody dared to offer us a ride. Consequently, we had no choice but to continue our arduous trudging and hope that soon the driver of a vehicle would take pity on us.

We walked on for a number of hours, without having any very clear idea of where we were, either looking straight ahead into the distance or down at the road at our feet. From time to time I sketched some piece of the captivating scenery, with my model, Christian Bach, in the foreground. My travelling companion, despairing at the slow rate at which we were making progress, came up with the ludicrous idea of making it look as if I was pregnant in the aim of awakening the slumbering compassion of the trap-drivers.

At first I protested and refused to acquiesce in this absurd proposal but as still not a single vehicle stopped to offer us a ride I gave up my resistance and let Christian create for me the tummy of a woman in the ninth month out of a bundle of clothes. The illusion of me as a woman with a very advanced pregnancy was apparently perfect, for shortly afterwards a trap pulled up beside us and its driver, an elegant lady aged about fifty, invited us in a friendly tone to step up into her trap. We naturally did not need asking twice, and during the journey to Bonn, which was where the lady lived, we talked about the "forthcoming birth of my child", and what name we had thought of giving it if it was a boy or a girl. The kindly lady, who really did believe that Christian and I were two lovers, gave us good advice about how to feed the baby and how children should best be brought up. When we alighted from the trap at her farm outside Bonn and prepared to continue our journey on foot, I felt for a moment as if I really was pregnant. I was soon brought back to reality, however, as Christian asked me to retain my artificial tummy in order to help us reach our destination more speedily. We started walking once more, but notwithstanding the advanced nature of my "pregnancy" not one vehicle halted, so we were left with no choice but to grit our teeth and march bravely on.

Towards midday, hungry and thirsty and with aching legs, we reached the beautiful town of Bonn. As we were drinking water from a well, three gendarmes armed with swords and pistols came up to us and in threatening tones ordered us to accompany them. Christian put on an expression of innocence and asked them for what reason, but one of the policemen just barked at him that he would find out soon enough. They prodded us in the back with their pistols and bellowed at Christian and me to start moving, and then under the gaping stares of the inhabitants of the town the gendarmes escorted us like two criminals to a dilapidated police station.

On arrival at the station a captain sporting a black walrus moustache informed us that we were being arrested for a number of serious robberies. This accusation shocked us, for although we had expected that we might be apprehended by the police on account of the unpaid hotel room in Cologne, we were guilty of no other offences. Christian raised loud protests against the accusations, and I tearfully professed our innocence.

Christian asked the captain what it was we were supposed to have done, and received the answer that several honest citizens along the Rhine had been robbed by a pregnant woman and her male companion, and that we would soon be brought face to face with those thus robbed. Hereupon I demonstratively removed my false stomach in order to prove to the police captain that I was not really pregnant, but in no way did this convince him of our innocence. On the contrary, he found it suspicious that I had been disguised in such a manner, and would not accept our explanation that I had only pretended to be pregnant in the aim of inducing passing vehicles to give us a ride. In his eyes we were the thieves and while he waited for "our victims" to arrive Christian and I were locked up in two adjacent cells which were fitted with bars and smelt strongly of urine. There was vermin crawling around on the dirty floor, and I shuddered with disgust and began weeping at being shut up in this repellent hole.

From the cell next to mine Christian tried to soothe me and keep my chin up. In a gentle voice he explained that we had obviously been mistaken for someone else, and comforted me by saying that the people who had been robbed would certainly confirm this to the police captain.

On hearing Christian's words I was able to calm myself a little; I looked around to find the place on the floor where there was the least filth, and sat down in a crouch to wait until Christian and I should be released. The hours passed by, without anyone appearing in the repulsive prison to let us out. I was about to give up hope, and firmly believed that we would be obliged to spend the night in this dungeon, when, at about eight o'clock in the evening, our cell doors were opened and Christian and I were ushered out by two policemen. They accompanied us into a room filled with shelves of documents.

After we had waited here in silence for about ten minutes the door was suddenly opened from the outside and in came, together with the gendarmes, a number of middle-aged men and women. The captain asked them something, pointing towards Christian and me. They all answered by shaking their heads, giving the captain to understand that we were not the two robbers the police had erroneously taken us to be.

A great weight was lifted from my heart, and I could see that Christian, too, was filled with relief. He smiled at me and I smiled back, and while the witnesses filed out of the room the captain came over to us and explained sullenly that we had been mistaken for a different couple, and that we were now free to go where we wanted. Not one word of regret passed over his lips, nor did he give the slightest apology for having detained us for so long even though we were innocent. We gave him a look of contempt and left the police station without saying a further word to anyone.

Our release from prison was far from signalling the end of our tribulations, and as we left the police station we found that heavy rain was falling over Bonn; this served as a reminder to us that it was evening and we once more had nowhere to lay our heads. In our search for shelter we wandered aimlessly around the dark and deserted streets of the town, at length finding an arched gateway under which we gained a modicum of shelter from the storm. In our sodden clothes we were preparing to spend an uncomfortable night out of doors, when all at once I remembered the three English gold sovereigns which my father had given me before we travelled to the Rhine as a secret reserve, which I should only use in the most severe emergency.

I had completely forgotten these three coins, but now, deeming that such a severe emergency was upon us, I extracted them from the small, buttoned-up pocket in my dress in which I had kept them. I showed the money to Christian and asked him, since I was not sure if the sovereign was legal tender in Germany: "Can English money be used to buy things in this country?" He looked at me and the gold coins in astonishment, and then nodded eagerly in confirmation, saying "Yes, of course, everybody accepts it!" After I had explained to Christian the reason for the sudden appearance of the money, we set off in search of a hotel.

Christian told me that in Germany the sovereign had a high value, so he thought that we did not have to content ourselves with a cheap hostelry: we could afford to spend the night in a good hotel. After our long trek along the dusty road and the time spent locked up in a filthy prison cell I wanted to taste again the luxury of cleanliness and orderliness, so I announced without further ado that only the best hotel in the town was good enough for us. Christian had no objections, and suggested the Grand Royal Hotel, which he knew about from hearsay.

We set off through the pouring rain and found the hotel situated in a large, fenced-in park looking over the Rhine. We saw that beyond the Rhine promenade there was a steam-ship landing stage. Passing through a wrought-iron gate we entered the park, which was illuminated with torches, and walked along a short gravel path between bushes and trees towards the castle-like hotel. Lights were shining in every window, which made the whole hotel look homely and welcoming.

As we came up to the entrance a hotel servant held the door open for us; on seeing the luxury of the interior I hesitated to go in, but my companion gave me a pat of encouragement on the back, so I gathered all my courage together and entered the hotel with Christian at my side, a self-confident expression on his face. Surrounded by elegant furniture, gilt-edged mirrors, glass and crystal, we strode, dripping wet, across the floor with its fine carpets towards Reception. I felt like something the cat had brought in, and I could see that the arrogant-looking head porter was thinking the same. Christian, however, did not let the man's looks of haughty disparagement disturb him: he presented himself and, as he wiped water from his face with his handkerchief, requested a double room. The porter, clearly repelled by our appearance, shook his head and began to tell us that he did not have any such room available when I put my three sovereigns on the counter in front of him and said, in English, that we would of course pay in advance. Hereupon the porter relaxed his haughty bearing, became extremely courteous, and suddenly discovered that he did, after all, have a double room which we could take.

After we had filled in the registration cards and completed all the formalities we borrowed dry clothes from him, went up to our delightful room on the second floor. We changed out of our wet garments, gave these to a hotel servant and charged him with ensuring that they were in good order by the following morning. We then made our way to the elegant dining room, in which only somewhat elderly guests were sitting eating, and to the accompaniment of their curious glances and whispered comments we ate a late dinner.

Over a tasty dish of pheasant, which was served on golden platters and with which we drank a good Rhenish wine out of elaborately cut glasses, we talked about the events of recent days, and also about things that had happened much further back in time. We started talking about our childhoods, and when I told Christian that from a young age I had been severely disciplined, he said this must be the cause of the fear and uncertainty in which he sensed that I had grown up. Surprised at his insight, I had to admit that he was right, since I had in fact had a hard childhood. My mother, who was a teacher before marrying Father, sees herself as being all but perfect and has never been able to imagine that I might want to be anything other than the image of her. She is flawless, and I must also strive so to be. Until I was six I felt that she gave me protection and comfort, but as soon as I started school she began to criticise and attack me. Mother's strongest motive forces are hate and contempt, which she feels towards everyone and everything and which have often caused her to lose her self-control completely.

I told Christian how my mother used to beat me for every smallest thing, and how, in order not to present her with reasons for punishing me even more, I had learned to adapt and be obedient. Perhaps, I mused aloud, I had only been so hard-working and obedient at school because I wanted my father finally to have something he could be proud about – we were all constantly obliged to listen to Mother telling him that there was nothing in his life he could feel proud about. Father, I continued my account to Christian, was the opposite of Mother, being of a quiet yet sociable nature, and it had always surprised me that the two of them had ever become a couple, bearing in mind the great differences in character that exist between them.

When I had finished recounting my history Christian told me about his childhood, and I learned that until he was six years old it had been very happy, but that thereafter it had been less joyful. The reason for this was the death of his much-loved twin brother Josef, who had died at the age of six from appendicitis. Sitting opposite me, Christian, with warmth in his voice, told me about his brother who, like him, had been fascinated by the stars, and even firmly believed that after his death he would become one of all the millions of stars in the night sky. Consequently, as Josef lay on his death bed, Christian had given his brother his word that on clear nights he would talk to him through the stars, and in this way stay in touch with him.

Christian confessed to me that ever since then he had often communicated with his dead brother, and said that he feared that because of this I might think he was mad. I of course assured my likeable companion that far from that, I found Christian's love for his brother very touching. I could see that my reaction pleased him greatly.

We finished our meal in silence, and when we had done so an elderly lady came up to our table. She had a round piece of wood in her hand, on which lay a large number of identical silver rings set with stones which shimmered in all the colours of the rainbow as the candle-light fell on them. The lady told us that the stones were of genuine Rhine crystal, and she was selling them at a very good price. I found the rings very beautiful, and when Christian asked if I would like one and would lend him the money to buy it, I immediately answered Yes. I selected a ring and slipped it onto the ring finger of my left hand. Christian asked the lady to put the cost of the ring on our room bill, and when the lady had moved on I thanked him for his lovely present and promised to treasure the ring as a memory of our odyssey. Christian replied, with a roguish winking of his eye, that I did not need to thank him – after all, it was not so difficult for him to make free with my money. Laughing, I had to agree with him. Thereupon our eyes met, and at this moment we both knew that we were about to fall in love with each other. However, we did not want, or were not able, to admit this to ourselves yet, so we began chatting about unimportant matters in order to distract ourselves from what we were really thinking and feeling. Christian nodded his head in the direction of a neighbouring table at which an elderly couple were sitting, and in a discreet whisper, told me that he always found it surprising how similar to each other married men and women grew over the years. I agreed with him, and said that I had made the same observation with regard to the owners of dogs and cats – that as time passed they came to resemble their pets more and more. Christian concurred, and once we had exhausted this subject and emptied our wine glasses we decided to retire.

We left the dining room, and mounted the elegantly ornamented staircase to our room on the second floor. Our room was very spacious, and filled with beautiful furniture and fine paintings. In addition to the wide bed there was a chest of drawers, a writing desk, an armchair and a chaise longue. After we had put on our night clothes Christian offered to sleep on the sofa, but I explained to him that as we had shared a bed on two previous occasions there was no reason why we should not do so a third time, and he came and joined me under the covers. Each of us modestly covered up in thick down-filled quilts, we lay beside each other in the bed, listening to the rain on the window. I spent a while writing up my diary, and Christian read a newspaper. I then wished him "good night" and put out the candle on the bedside table. The torches in the park cast a faint light through our open curtains, illuminating the bed with a weak flicker. All we could hear was the rustling of the wind and the pattering sound of the rain, until from beside me in the bed Christian suddenly asked: "Tell me something about your Henry, Miss Idilia".

I was taken aback by his question, and at first did not know what to answer. Regaining my composure I retorted, "What do you want me to tell you about him?".

"What kind of person he is", returned Christian, whereupon I began to describe Henry, at first hesitantly, but with increasing fluency. I depicted him as a handsome, cultivated and ambitious nobleman, a man with political ambitions who would certainly one day be a highly ranked statesman.

Christian did not seem to be very impressed by my description of Henry, and asked again, almost with a touch of impatience in his voice, what kind of person he was, not what kind of politician or nobleman. Notwithstanding the fact that I had ended my connection with Henry owing to his constant unfaithfulness and unbearable arrogance, I portrayed him as a better person than he is in reality, with the result that when I had finished Christian had fallen completely still and silent.

By the time I realised that I had made a mistake in praising Henry to the skies, and tried to correct the impression I had given by describing his worst sides, it was too late: in Christian's eyes he was the loser with regard to me, and Henry was the winner, try as I might to convince my companion next to me in bed that this was a misunderstanding. All my words were in vain – the pleasant mood that had prevailed between the two of us evaporated, and I deeply regretted that thanks to my unthinking tongue I had thrown away the opportunity of getting even closer to Christian. I was painfully aware that the distance I had put between us would remain for the rest of this night, so there was nothing left for us to do but to wish each other a good night and pull the covers up to our ears. We turned our backs to each other and tried to go to sleep, but our heads were so full of spinning thoughts that neither of us could sleep. We tossed and turned but did not say a word to each other, until finally we were both overtaken by sleep towards morning.

Wednesday, 11th June 1851
I dreamt that I was locked inside a prison cell, and that I stood shaking the bars and desperately appealing to be let out. Christian was with me in the cell; he was sitting in his leather armchair, holding a fishing rod in his hand and gazing up at the cell window, where the starry night sky was to be seen. All at once the door was flung open from the outside and into the cell came Henry, in the same uniform as lieutenant Wiessel had worn. At the sight of my former betrothed I burst into tears and cowered backwards into the cell, but Henry took a rough hold of my arm, pulled me over to the bunk, and lay down on his back. He then drew me down over him and began intensively stroking my back. I found myelf enjoying Henry's rough yet tender attentions and asked him to continue, while Christian watched us with a sad expression

on his face, swinging a handbell in his hand.

I awoke, and in the distance I could hear the character-istic ringing sound of a ship's bell announcing departure; at the same time, as I lay in bed I discovered that Christian, fast asleep, was holding me tightly in his arms. I smiled at this discovery, feeling no indignation, although I did try carefully to extract myself from his embrace. My efforts woke him, and when he saw how close he had come to me while we slept he apologised and instantly withdrew his arm, assuring me that he had not done it on purpose. I told him that I believed him, whereupon he quickly jumped up out of bed and as quickly as he could began to dress him-self, while I watched him, amused. It being already nine o'clock I too got out of bed, and once a hotel servant had brought us our washed and ironed clothes we dressed our-selves and descended to the dining room to eat a late breakfast. While we ate we learned from a waiter that at eleven o'clock a steamer would be leaving for Coblenz, and we decided that we would travel with that ship. I was worried that we would not have enough money, but when Christian paid our hotel bill with my sovereigns he was given so much change that we were easily able to afford two tickets.

It was a fine, refreshing morning, and I was looking forward to all I would experience in the course of the day. While we waited for our ship, Christian and I strolled along the Rhine promenade, together with other tourists, most of them English. I was surprised by the civilised behaviour that prevailed in Bonn, where the men held themselves with dignity and the women conducted themselves with grace. We saw nice-looking children out walking with their tastefully attired parents, and people carrying brightly coloured parasols. Elderly ladies and young girls looked at us in curiosity and gave us a friendly "Guten Morgen". Alongside us the Rhine flowed with a throaty, muttering sound, the sky was an azure blue, and away to the east we could see a long chain of mountains, on one of the lofty peaks of which there perched a ruined castle.

8

A SIGNAL SHOT in the distance heralded the arrival of a steam-ship, and shortly before 11am the *Victoria*, coming from the direction of Cologne, reached the landing stage at Bonn. It was a small passenger paddle-steamer, decked with pennants and crowded with passengers, a number of whom went ashore in Bonn where carriers with handcarts were waiting to receive them. Scarcely had Christian and I had time to go aboard and find an unoccupied place to sit, before the steamer cast off again and once more began pounding upstream with smoke gushing from its funnel.

It is really only at Bonn that the beautiful Rhineland region commences, taking the form of a wide gorge between hills and mountains leading up to the Mosel at Coblenz, the destination of our journey. Every moment aboard the *Victoria* presented some new interesting sight to our view. We saw cheerful-looking villages, water-mills, and mountains piled up in layers which on one side cast their shadow over the river while on the other side the hills stood bathed in bright sunshine. We sailed past the "Siebengebirge" where, according to legend, the castle of the dragon-slayer Siegfried stood. As we passed this point one or two passengers on our ship fired their pistols, and the bangs, like the pounding of the ship's rudder, were returned from the cliffs with a sevenfold echo – the name "Siebengebirge" means "Seven Mountains". As I gazed up in fascination at the ruined castle on the summit of "Drachenfels" (which means "Dragon Mountain"), Lord Byron's lines from "Childe Harold" sprang to my mind, and I quoted them to Christian:

> *The castled crag of Drachenfels*
> *Frowns o'er the wide and winding Rhine,*
> *Whose breast of waters broadly swells*
> *Between the banks which bear the vine,*
> *And hills all rich with blossomed trees,*
> *And fields which promise corn and wine,*
> *And scattered cities crowning these,*
> *Whose far white walls along them shine,*
> *Have strewed a scene, which I should see*
> *With double joy wert thou with me!*

My travelling companion heard me patiently out and then applauded my oratory, before enquiring ironically, in the belief that I had spoken the poem with him in mind, if I found his presence a source of double joy. With a laugh I said that I did indeed, keeping to myself the fact that I had actually thought of Henry while reciting the poem, since I had sent it to him in a letter I had written in Coblenz during my first visit to the Rhineland last year. Not knowing that my former fiancé was still occupying my mind Christian smiled warmly at me. Wanting to change the subject, I asked him what the difference was between the German words *"Burg"* and *"Schloß"*, since they were both translated by the same English word, castle. He proceeded cheerfully to instruct me that while it was possible to live a good life in a *"Burg"*, this kind of castle was above all a fortification, a construction conceived for defence. A *"Schloß"* on the other hand, he continued, was conceived as a residence. Here life was much more pleasant to bear, since a *"Schloß"* was built with the sole purpose of adding a measure of luxury to everyday life; a *"Schloß"* was not a building in which one simply lived, but in which one truly resided.

Listening to Christian's description I could not help thinking of Henry again, who himself lived in such a milieu, and once more I came to the conclusion that I needed no luxury, and no *"Schloß"*, in order to be happy. To lead a modest life, with the occasional journey during which I can paint and draw to my heart's content: that, Gwen, is enough to make me happy. Neither must the man of my dreams be a millionaire or an aristocrat; it is more than enough for me if he has intelligence and humour and can make me laugh. Christian, I thought to myself, is such a man, and in the course of our long journey up the Rhine he has given repeated proof of this fact.

We had been sailing up the Rhine for a number of hours, betwixt mountains with vineyards on their sides, and pretty villages and small towns, when our steamer, the *Victoria*, arrived at the old town of Andernach in the late afternoon, coming in to moor on the left bank in order to set down a number of passengers and take aboard others. Andernach lay at the foot of a high, forest-covered mountain on the side of which, in the midst of a number of farmhouses, a mighty ruined fortress and a church with four spires could be seen.

Christian and I stood at the ship's rail, watching all the bustle on the shore, when he suddenly caught sight of something amid all the goings-on which captured his attention. He was so absorbed in what it was he was observing that he did not hear me when I asked, my curiosity aroused, what it was that was so interesting over on the shore. It was only after I had repeated my question that

Christian emerged from his state of rapt concentration, and nodded towards where a black-haired man aged about twenty was standing next to a pregnant girl: "That must be the couple the police took us for," he said.

The two of them looked like gypsies; they were dressed in ragged clothes and were holding out their hands to beg from the passengers who were leaving the ship to go aland. The sight seemed to awaken sympathy in Christian, and although the ship's bell was just ringing to announce the ship's imminent departure he wanted to go quickly ashore and warn the couple that the police were looking for them. Before I could do anything to prevent him he hurried over the gangway, went up to the couple and began talking to them. Their conversation seemed to go on for an eternity, and when Christian waved to me to join them I shook my head vigorously, since I did not want the experience yet again of missing our boat. However, when the ship's crew made ready to pull in the gangway and I saw that Christian would be unable to get back onto the boat, I snatched up our luggage and stormed angrily off the ship. It felt as if Christian's spontaneous ideas were going to prevent us from ever reaching that destination, and I walked up to him ready to give him a piece of my furious mind.

However, as I approached he gave me such a friendly smile that my anger immediately blew over. Christian introduced the couple to me as Edith and Jean, and as I, rather hesitatingly, took their outstretched hands they affirmed in broken English that they were not thieves at all, but innocent circus artists from France who had left their troupe and were therefore penniless. As their bad luck would have it, they both complained, the people along the Rhine had wrongly accused them of being thieves, which made it impossible for them to earn any honest money and had forced them to take to begging as their only means of survival. Edith told us that she was six months pregnant, and Jean added that she had not had a proper meal for several days.

In return for the money Christian had given them the girl was set on telling our fortunes, and it was for this reason that Christian had let the steamer sail off without us and deprived me of the opportunity of soon being reunited with my family in Coblenz. That did not seem to bother Christian in the slightest, so intent was he on finding out what the future held in store for us. I for my part showed no interest in this, since as far as I am concerned fortune-telling is nothing but humbug, and what was more I had no confidence in the clairvoyant abilities of the girl, who was scarcely older than me. I was therefore at first reluctant to let her read my palm, although in the end I yielded to Christian's persuasions.

We went to sit down a little way off from the landing stage on a patch of grass, where Edith began by reading Christian's palm, prophesying a long life, with great success in his work but great sorrow in his private life.

Thereafter it was my turn, and when I held out my hand to Edith she started in fear at what she saw. She tried to conceal her reaction from me but I had noticed it well enough, and when I asked her what the future looked like for me she tried to talk her way out of it with a woolly account of some long journey I would make, at the end of which I would come to an important realisation. This prophecy was no use to me at all, since I was already on such a journey, during the course of which I would obviously gather some kind of experience or another. One did not need to be endowed with clairvoyant powers to work out that much, I intimated derisively to the girl. I could see from Christian's expression that he too was disappointed in the pregnant girl's fortune-telling, and I urged him to make ready to leave.

We bade the pitiful couple farewell, and they continued on their way on foot, while Christian and I set off in search of a stagecoach with which we could resume our journey to Coblenz. As we did so I brooded over the girl's reaction at what she saw written in my palm, and, with a sense of unease, tried in vain to think of what it could be that she had seen. When I mentioned her prophecies to Christian he dismissed them contemptuously as nonsense, and with a feeling of relief I concurred in his judgement.

We sat near the landing stage for a good while, waiting for the appearance of some means of conveyance to Coblenz. At length a diligence came along, and we left

Andernach and headed south in the glow of the setting sun. Besides Christian and me there was one other passenger in the coupé of the diligence, a fair-haired Dutchman of about the same age as my travelling companion. After we had introduced ourselves to each other in English, and learnt that the Dutchman was a cabinet maker who was in Germany on holiday, the two men continued their conversation while I tried to rest a little.

That was however easier said than done, since our conveyance was uncomfortable and the road to Coblenz most treacherous. At first we made but slow progress, since stones, puddles and deep sand hindered the vehicle, and to our alarm on a number of occasions the coach was in peril of turning over. The closer we drew to Coblenz the more made-up the road was, and towards the end of our journey it was surfaced entirely with unhewn stones, with the result that we passengers were shaken most cruelly and left black and blue. The uneven nature of the road did not however prevent our taciturn, stubborn coachman from actually increasing speed, and all the angry words we directed at him for his inconsiderate driving bounced off him like hailstones from a tiled roof.

The long journey and the annoyance we had been caused by the driver had left me feeling tired, and at length I fell asleep. I was soon, however, woken again by the jolting and rumbling of the stagecoach, but I kept my eyes closed in the hope that I would soon be able to doze off again. At this point I heard the Dutchman ask Christian if I was his bride-to-be, to which Christian replied, "No, I'm betrothed to someone else."

Christian's answer came as a shock to me, since I had believed all along that he had not been tied to a woman for a long time – at least, that is how I had understood what he had said to me in Holland when we first met, three days ago. I made sure that I gave no outward sign of how agitated I was, and pretended to be still asleep, so that I might learn more about this relationship. To my regret Christian did not reveal any more about it, so throughout the rest of the journey I was filled with only one single wish, and that was that we should arrive in Coblenz as soon as possible so that I could get away from my deceitful travelling companion and never have to see him again.

It was evening when the coachman blew his horn to signal that we would soon be arriving in Coblenz. Shortly afterwards we entered the town and the diligence drove through the narrow streets and alleys to the Coblenzer Hof hotel, where I knew that my father had taken rooms for our family. Christian, quite the gentleman, helped me as I stepped down from the coach, asking me as he did so if I would like to join him at a summer festival in Oberlahnstein next Saturday.

In answer I pressed into his hand the ring he had given me in Bonn and said in a cold, impersonal tone that he could go to the festival with his fiancée and did not need me. Thereupon Christian began staring alternately at me and the ring in his hand, and was clearly so taken aback by my unexpected sally that for a moment he was as if paralysed and unable to speak. He then recovered himself somewhat and said that everything was a big misunderstanding, and tried to give the ring back to me. I refused to take it back, and told Christian he could give it to his fiancée, to which he replied that he had bought the ring for me and nobody else. Not moved by his words, I retorted that he had bought it with my money, and that therefore it was I who should decide what was to be done with it. I snatched up my effects, and began striding rapidly towards the hotel. Behind me I heard the coachman mumbling something in an impatient tone, and then Christian shouted out "Please forgive me, Miss Idilia, but I meant well, really I did!"

His apology surprised me, and as I turned round I saw him standing in the door of the stagecoach, waving to me with a pained smile on his face. Then the coach moved off, leaving me behind, lost in thought.

I entered the hotel and asked the owner after my family. He told me that they were in the lounge, and as I entered that room I saw my parents and brother and sister sitting at a long table, eating a meal. When they saw me their faces lit up; they jumped up from their chairs, and each embraced me in turn and said how pleased they were that I was back with them. I then sat down with them at their table and recounted the adventures I had had since being separated from them. They were so happy to see me again, safe and sound, that they forgave me my long absence.

It was noticeable to me that Mother and Father seemed to be on good terms with each other again, and that my brother George was much more relaxed than he had been on board the steamer. I mentioned these observations to my sister Mary later on, as we were readying ourselves for bed, and she said that Father had given his rival, the German wine-grower, a good thrashing because of his audacious flirting with Mother, and that since then Mother had been very friendly towards our father. With regard to George, Mary could tell me that he had mustered the courage to speak to the girl with fair plaits who had so captivated him, and that, as their ways had parted at Coblenz, he had even exchanged addresses with her.

Mary also told me that she had taken charge of Christian's travelling bag when he had left it on the ship, and that she had stowed it under our bed in the hotel room we were sharing. I praised her for her actions, and promised her that I would return it to Christian when the opportunity arose – although I as yet had no idea how I should go about doing this. Mary herself was very much taken with the country and its inhabitants; she had resolved to learn German and at a later date, when she was old enough, she wished to return on her own to the Rhineland and explore it at her own leisure. I encouraged her in these resolutions and thought to myself, as we lay next to each other in the bed, that our journey up the Rhine had ended propitiously for my parents and my brother and sister, if not for myself.

Once more I had placed my faith in a man, and once more that man had led me up the garden path. I felt so bitterly disappointed that I started to weep. I cried silently into my pillow, in order that Mary should not hear my despair. She fell asleep without having noticed my sadness, whereupon I rose from the bed, and sat down at the little writing table in our room and there, by the light of a single wretched tallow candle, I wrote my diary.

Thursday, 12th June 1851
During the night I dreamt that I was pregnant, and was fleeing from the police together with Christian. We were riding on a black horse, and I urged him not to ride so fast since I was afraid of losing my baby. However Christian, who in my dream was wearing the uniform of a German stagecoach driver, paid no heed to my entreaty; indeed, he spurred the horse on to even greater speed, and I was so badly shaken that I feared that at any moment I would have to give birth to my child. I boxed Christian in the back and shouted at him in panic to stop, but he rode on

without listening to me. I threw myself therefore off the horse and landed heavily, after traversing a considerable distance through the air, on the foredeck of a steam-ship. Lying on the deck I bore my child, observed unemotionally by Christian who sat in a leather armchair smoking a long clay pipe. When I lifted my howling, blood-covered baby I saw that it had the face of my sister Mary.

I awoke and saw Mary lying next to me in bed crying hysterically. Sobbing, she told me that she had been having a nightmare, in which she had found me dead on the stairs of the hotel, and which had felt just like reality. I embraced and comforted Mary, and after we had sat for a while on the bed, holding each other tightly, my dear younger sister grew calm again.

My parents had set this Thursday aside for having a close look at Coblenz, since on our journey to the Rhineland last year, the town had only been a stopping point on our travels. The town is characterised by black walls, and is situated between dark mountains, the countryside along the river, and broad, level fields. With its mighty fortress Ehrenbreitstein, perched in splendour on a high crag, the town has the appearance of having seen grandeur in the past. It is at Coblenz that the river Mosel flows into the Rhine, and the surrounding countryside is filled with villages, ruins, castles and rose-coloured churches. Dressed in our best summer clothes we strolled through the beautiful town looking at churches and old houses.

At midday we entered an inn, where we orderd the regional speciality, black pudding with a purée of potatoes and apples, with which my parents drank a bottle of wine and my brother and sister and I lemonade. After our meal we walked along the delightful Rhine promenade, where there were row upon row of the most magnificent carriages, throngs of both male and female riders, and crowds of elegantly dressed men and women on foot proudly displaying their diamonds, gold watches, chains and other treasures.

Everybody was gaping at everybody else, and since it could be seen that we were strangers to the town and therefore ignorant of the customs and manners there, the young snobs began inspecting us through glasses, and passing comment with pitying smiles. As we had no wish to continue as an object of ridicule, we left the Rhine promenade and betook ourselves to other parts of the town, where we were less at risk of being mocked by the snooty, well-to-do denizens of the town. We visited a museum displaying the complete works of the famous artist Albrecht Dürer, and then continued our explorations in that part of Coblenz which is situated on the right bank of the Rhine. Here we visited Ehrenbreitstein, a crag close to the river which is a natural fortress, and is therefore known as the "German Gibraltar". At the foot of this mountain there is a cluster of arsenals and magazines, whose fine portals and columns made them look like buildings belonging to a castle. This district, a friendly passer-by told us, is also the location of Coblenz's artists colony, but however much we kept a lookout we did not catch sight of a single artist. Since, as I do not need to tell you, I consider myself to be an artist I felt a particular interest in this picturesque spot, and I made a sketch or two, being observed the while, at first with interest but then with boredom, by the other members of my family. We then continued on our way, eagerly anticipating all the new sights which would present themselves to us.

As the sun started to sink in the West we had seen enough for one day and began the long walk home. On reaching our hotel, it was still quite light and warm so we sat in the hotel's wine garden where, together with the other guests, we had an enjoyable evening meal.

The friendly hotel-keeper had organised tickets for the Coblenz town theatre, to which my parents travelled by coach after our meal, while my brother and sister and I remained at the hotel, passing the time with various board and card games. We then retired to our rooms, and for a long time after Mary had fallen asleep and my parents had returned to the hotel I sat at the writing table and wrote up my diary.

Friday, 13th June 1851

Despite the fact that I went to bed late yesterday I woke at 4am, roused by the crowing of cockerels, and was unable to go back to sleep. I suddenly came to think of Christian, and it occurred to me that, strangely enough, I had not thought of him once throughout the whole of yesterday. Now my thoughts were occupied with him all the more, and I tried to find an answer to the question of why he had not been honest to me; had he pretended not to be engaged any longer thinking that this would make it easier for him to win me over? Or was he only outwardly still engaged while inwardly regarding the betrothal as having been terminated a long time since?

I twisted and turned the arguments in my head as I lay in my bed, but came to no definite answer. I tried to imagine what kind of girl Christian had bound himself to; I wondered if she was similar to me in appearance or character, or if she was exactly my opposite. Although I did not know his fiancée and had never seen her, in my mind I jealously endowed her with all the worst characteristics I could think of. I thought she must surely be old, ugly and completely lacking in charm: nothing else was possible. As soon as I had thought this, however, I rejected it, realising that it was an absurd idea to imagine the attractive and charming Christian together with a girl of such a description.

Obviously, the contrary was most likely to be the case;

for a man of Christian's stature nothing other than a girl of outstanding beauty, intelligence and worldly sophistication could come into question. This thought released a new wave of hot jealousy within me, and I realised, although I had not wanted to admit it to myself up to now, that Christian was more to me than a casual holiday acquaintance of the kind that one forgets as soon as one's ways have parted.

I resolved to ascertain whether Christian felt the same way as I did, how close his relationship with his betrothed was, and if he was ready to leave her for my sake. Now, I could not gain any answer to these questions in Coblenz; I had to betake myself to his home town of Oberlahnstein, which is only a few miles distant. In order to get there I needed the permission and co-operation of my parents, and being certain that they would not allow me to go and visit Christian on my own I decided that the best expedient would be to persuade them to undertake a family outing to Oberlahnstein.

I suggested this destination to my parents at breakfast, and was delighted when, rather than objecting, they agreed that since we had not yet seen the town a visit there was long overdue. We learned from the hotel owner that Oberlahnstein also has a fine old ruined castle, which is called "Lahneck" and is well worth a visit. The friendly man suggested that we might like to spend the night in a well-known inn on the banks of the Lahn, close to where it joins the Rhine, and we found this an excellent idea. In eager anticipation we packed some provender for the journey, and a change of clothing, before setting off on foot.

The weather was glorious, although the road we followed out of Coblenz was extremely poor, so we made but laborious progress. To all sides we saw fruit trees decked with blossom, and in the vineyards we saw workers pruning the vines. The sun blazed down on us from a clear blue sky and we had to stop frequently to wipe the perspiration from our faces and refresh ourselves with a sip of water. From time to time I paused to sketch houses, trees or attractive landscape scenes, finding myself as I did so surrounded by swarms of mosquitoes, bees and colourful butterflies. The higher up we came the more captivating was the view that presented itself to us. To the right we saw the "Stolzenfels" fort, and on the left the ruin of Lahneck, both of them perching on high crags. Along the river Lahn we could see the two towns of Niederlahnstein and Oberlahnstein (*"Nieder"* meaning "Lower" and *"Ober"* meaning "Upper"), which were linked to each other by an avenue of trees. Next to them, on the right-hand bank of the river, two dilapidated spires rose upwards from a house of worship, which according to our travel guide was the "Johanniskirche", or Church of St John.

We took our time walking, and were in no hurry to reach our destination, since the weather was magnificent, and the surroundings likewise. We climbed along an old path, laid with rough stones as steps, up the side of a steep hill, and met a field warden who greeted us in a friendly manner. In the midst of the vines we saw scarecrows and heard the buzzing of the flies, singing of birds and cooing of doves. After a steep climb up through vines and bushes we arrived, breathless, at the grass-covered top of the hill, and stood to admire the prospect at our feet with the verdant countryside and the glittering Rhine. The ringing of bells from villages and the lowing of cattle in the fields were borne up to us on the wind. I captured the glorious panorama in my sketch-book, and after a leisurely picnic, during which we fortified ourselves with the cold roast chicken and wine we had brought with us, we resumed our trek through the Rhineland countryside, which was redolent with the scent of flowers and wild herbs.

9

IN THE LATE AFTERNOON, we reached the small town of Niederlahnstein, which made a peaceful and sleepy impression as we approached, with its churches, carved gables, and roofs with weather vanes. As we entered the picturesque town a flock of geese came hissing towards us, but the young girl who was tending them shooed them to one side so that we could pass. The elderly residents we encountered doffed their hats in greeting, and the children playing in the narrow streets stood aside to afford us passage.

Father asked a young man, who was a baker, where the reputed inn on the Lahn could be found; the young man pointed out the direction we should take, and Father thanked him for his kindness with a German coin. On reaching the inn, an attractive old half-timbered building from which a semicircular tower projected and which was once a toll-house, we were welcomed by the stout landlord, who spoke good English. He proudly showed us the house, and we took two rooms, one for my parents and one for my brother and sister and myself.

We then took a walk along the Lahn, watching the fishermen and boatmen as they went about their work, and as the sun dropped behind the roofs of Niederlahnstein we saw the ferryman rowing some late passengers over the Lahn in his boat. In the distance we heard the ringing of church bells, and mist rose up from the river, veiling from view the houses of Niederlahnstein where they had been visible just a few minutes before. Above the upper edge of the mist we could see the ruined castle of Lahneck high on its crag, and above the castle a lone predatory bird circled in the sky. It was cool out of doors and we started shivering, so we decided to return to our inn. We entered the inn to find the air filled with the smell of frying fat, and we saw the landlady standing at a fireplace frying red-speckled trout over the glowing embers. We sat down at a long table where there were still some empty places, and while the meal was being prepared I sketched the good woman at her work.

After a tasty evening meal we remained seated for a long while, talking about all we had seen during the day over wine and lemonade, and then listening to an old, one-legged violinist who, in return for a modest gratuity entertained us throughout the evening. The only thing that disturbed our enjoyment somewhat was a little old man sitting at one of the neighbouring tables, who kept clearing his throat at regular intervals, and voiding his nose with the aid of his fingers.

The ringing of a bell announced that it was closing time, we mounted the stairs to our rooms on the second floor. As is usual in Germany, they were clean and tidy, but the quilts were far too warm for summer nights and the beds were so short that only very small people or children could find them sufficiently roomy. Whereas George and Mary fell asleep as soon as they had laid themselves in bed, I sat down at the little writing table in our room and, by the light of an oil lamp, wrote my diary.

Saturday, 14th June 1851
The air was humid and at about 1 am – I was still sitting at the writing table, writing these lines – I heard distant thunder. The peals of thunder grew ever closer, ever louder, and the lightning seemed to flash right outside my window. The flashes of lightning illuminated the ruin of Lahneck castle, making it look even more forbidding than it had done by day. It started to rain, and soon the rain and the thunderstorm were so heavy that I no longer dared to sit next to the window. I closed my diary, removed my outer clothes down to my petticoat, and after extinguish-

ing the lamp slipped into the bed in which my brother and sister were already deep in sleep. I pulled the thick quilt up to my ears and hoped fervently that the terrible thunder would soon abate. While the elemental forces raged all around the inn, inside in the stuffy room I lay in the warm bed remembering and contemplating everything I had experienced on my journey and with Christian. My final thoughts before I fell asleep were of him, and when I awoke the following morning my first thoughts were of him too.

The night-time thunderstorm had purged the air, and when I opened the window at about five o'clock in the morning, a fresh, cool wind blew into my face. The wind had cleared away the rain clouds from the night, but left the mist behind, which was still draped in veils over the river and the adjacent countryside. Before long, however, it began to disperse, and through a gap I could see, on the other side of the river, the ruined castle of Lahneck, with the rays of the rising sun falling in through its empty door and window openings. Dawn broke and the sky lightened, but everyone in the inn was still asleep. I dressed and left the room, and went out in order to be able to enjoy the beauty alone and undisturbed. As I walked down to the river the mist rose from the water, and as I reached the bank the sun was shining down on me. I looked all around to assure myself that no other person was in the vicinity, and strained to listen but heard no sound other than the gentle lapping of the Lahn and the rustling of the reeds. Certain that I was quite alone I quickly removed my petticoat and waded out, fully naked, into the cold water, which at this point, was rather shallow.

Following my refreshing morning dip I hurriedly dressed myself again and returned to the inn, which by now was full of life – although my family was the exception, since neither my parents nor my brother or sister were yet to be seen. I elected to eat breakfast without waiting for them; my little early-morning excursion had left me hungry and thirsty, so I sat down at table with the other guests. Since they all only spoke German we could not converse with each other, so we contented ourselves with friendly smiles and nods and then proceeded to partake of our breakfast in silence. The meal consisted of milky coffee and a bread roll, together with porridge served with milk and cinnamon. I chose not to take the coffee, and had porridge and a cup of tea, which however had a dreadful tarry taste.

The inn was an agreeable place in which to spend time – it was interesting simply to watch the guests who came and went, or to look through the window towards the Lahn, where there was an uninterrupted movement of boats and ships, both down the river and also, with the help of draught horses, upstream.

My parents, who came downstairs with my brother and sister at about 9 am, had other plans for the day than merely to sit in the inn watching the world go by. They were very eager to get to know the surrounding countryside, and after they had eaten breakfast, watched by me, we betook ourselves in the glorious weather to what is called "All Saints' Mount" (in German "Allerheiligen-Berg"), an old place of pilgrimage above the town. There we looked at a chapel and took a long walk through vineyards and fields, and along the pretty river Lahn, where at one point we tasted the water of a spring from which the water emerged aerated. This caused me to think of Christian, and I recalled his invitation to the summer festival, which was to take place today in the neighbouring town of Oberlahnstein. I was undecided as to whether I should attend the festivity or not, and resolved that I would make up my mind as soon as I knew what plans my parents had for the afternoon and evening.

As the hour approached one o'clock of the afternoon we made our way back to the inn; we sat at a long table in the garden behind the house together with the other guests, and enjoyed an excellent meal, consisting of meat broth as a first course, with the main dish being a kind of potato dumpling served with meat. The adults drank a dry table wine with their meal, and the younger guests drank lemonade. We were just eating our dessert, a fruit compote, when from the street we heard the repeated blowing of a horn. Shortly afterwards a stagecoach halted beside the inn and a tall, blond male passenger wearing a hat climbed down from the conveyance. The postillion handed him a travelling bag, receiving a gratuity in thanks, and then the new arrival entered the inn via the main entrance. A few moments later he appeared in the door to the garden, and on seeing us removed his hat. At this I recognised the man as Henry, my former fiancé, and I can assure you Gwen, my dear friend, that the sight of him left me utterly thunderstruck. In the course of my adventure-filled journey along the Rhine I had come to expect that well-nigh anything could happen, but never would I have expected my former betrothed to appear in this spot. I wished nothing more than to be swallowed up by the ground, but he had already made me out from where he stood, and waved to me with a smile. I gave a forced smile in reply, and my mother turned round to see who, or what, it was that caused me to react in such a way. When she caught sight of Henry she called out his name, her face beaming with delight, and rose from her chair with her hand stretched out so that she could be the first to greet him. Henry shook her hand nonchalantly, said "Hello" to the others sitting at the table, and then came over to me and embraced me. Still shocked, I asked him "What are you doing here?", to which he replied in a honeyed voice, giving me a kiss on the cheek, "I've come to visit you, my dearest".

When I then asked him how he could know that we were in Niederlahnstein, in this particular inn, he answered that the owner of our hotel in Coblenz had told him. He had found out that that was where we were going while still in Edinburgh, from our maid Rose. After my family and I had left Scotland for Germany and as soon as he had ascertained what our destination was, he had immediately followed us, taking the first train and steamer he could. He had however not succeeded in catching up with us although, he assured us, he had been very close to doing so on a number of occasions. I was glad that he had not, and gave an inward sigh of relief, since I could not conceive what would have happened if he had found me together with Christian on a steam-ship or in a hotel.

As to the reason for his sudden appearance among us, Henry said that after I had left for the Rhine he had missed me very much, and not been able to bear being without me. He then turned to my parents and my brother and sister and hypocritically begged them to excuse what he called his "unannounced visit to their holiday resort".

I found his confession embarrassing in front of all the people there, and I could see that my father and brother and sister also found the situation awkward. My mother, on the other hand, was quite clearly delighted at Henry's words; she nodded in agreement, beaming all over her face, and I thought to myself that it was a very long time since I had seen her like this. In her eyes the fact that Henry had come all this way to see me signalled the beginning of a reconciliation between us, and she obviously hoped that we would in time resume our engagement. In her joyful excitement Mother assured Henry that we were all very pleased that he had chosen to visit us, but when I gave her to understand, by means of a disapproving look, that she could speak for herself but not for me, she grew somewhat embarrassed, cleared her throat and asked Henry if he would care to sit down with us. In a brusque tone she told George, who was sitting next to me, to make room, but Henry shook his head and said that he would like to talk to me alone for a moment. Before I had time to raise any objections he tugged me away from the bench on which I was sitting, begged everybody else's pardon for the disturbance he had caused, and left the garden, taking me with him with his arm laid possessively around my waist.

I accompanied him reluctantly, and as we made our way towards the bank of the Lahn Henry averred that he was still deeply in love with me and that he regretted having been unfaithful to me. When I explained that his realisations had come too late he would have nothing of it, retorting that it is never too late to atone for the mistakes one has made. To this I answered that he had insulted and injured me to such a serious degree that he could not put everything right that easily, whereupon he took hold of both of my hands and kissed them, looking me deep in the eyes and begging me a thousand times to forgive him. Torn between conflicting feelings, I stood there on the river bank, listening with half an ear to Henry's professions of love and vows of fidelity. Exhausted by his gushing torrent of words and feeling cornered by his persuasive oratory, I promised to give him one final chance. On hearing this he fell to his knees and vowed, his voice thick with emotion, that he would never disappoint me again. I would have liked to believe him, but too often have I had the experience of his breaking his promises to think that this time things might be different. However, since I did not wish to find myself at a later date reproaching myself for having prevented a reconciliation between us, I resolved to accept his promise for the time being, but to put his steadfastness to the test this very weekend. I requested him to rise from his embarrassing position of genuflection in front of me, and he hastened to comply with my wish. We then returned to the inn, where Henry took a single room for one night only, since he was expecting that we would be returning to our hotel in Coblenz on Sunday.

As we sat drinking coffee in the garden of the inn beside the Lahn together with my parents and brother and sister, we agreed that we would spend the afternoon sightseeing in Oberlahnstein. The following day, Sunday, after going to church we would all make the journey to Bad Ems where we would visit the famous medicinal baths.

At about three o'clock of the Saturday afternoon Anton Douqué, the Niederlahnstein ferryman, rowed us in his little boat over the Lahn and set us down on the shore by the ferryhouse. We were now in the Duchy of Hessen/

Nassau, and, passing a high mountain with the ruined castle of Lahneck on its peak, we walked towards the town of Oberlahnstein, situated on a level stretch of land with the Rhine flowing past.

Following a long walk through cultivated fields and past orchards of fruit and nut trees we reached a large gate, through which we entered the town with its pointed gabled roofs, tall, dark walls, and spires and churches. We walked along the deserted main street, onto which narrow and even narrower alleys opened, and looked with interest at all there was to see. After we had looked at the Church of St Martin, the rather dilapidated town hall on the market square, a well pump and the old toll-tower, we heard cheerful music somewhere close at hand.

Drawn on by the sound, we found that the music was coming from a large courtyard which was decked with flowers and leafy branches, and which was filled with long benches and tables at which the residents of the town were seated with glasses of wine and tankards of beer in front of them. In the midst of this gathering five musicians were playing next to a dance floor of wooden boarding, on which couples of all ages were whirling around in time to the music. At the sight of all the people enjoying themselves I remembered Christian's invitation to this festival, and since I had no wish for him to see me here in the company of Henry I tried to move quickly on. However, Henry thought we really should have something to drink, and before I could turn around he had propelled me into an unoccupied seat and invited my parents and brother and sister to sit down beside us. Since there were so many people here, whose language and customs they did not understand, my family did not want to stay. I felt the same way as they did. But Henry, with the wordy support of Mother, urged me to stay and take part in the dancing. Unable to defend myself against this alliance of the two of them I remained seated, and after Henry had promised my parents that he would return me safe and sound and at not too late an hour to our inn in Niederlahnstein, my family left us.

Once they had disappeared into the throng of people filling the courtyard Henry bought us a jug of wine from a waitress. He poured out two glasses, raised his, said "To your health", and then emptied the glass in a single draught. Before I had even tasted my wine he had refilled his glass to the brim. Previous experience had taught me that when Henry starts behaving like this it always ends in drunkenness with associated unpleasantness, so I begged him to be a little more careful with the wine. Henry merely waved my concern aside, saying that it would take more than watery vinegar like that to knock him off his feet. I was not at all convinced that this was the case, but decided not to try and order him to stop drinking, since that would only have irritated him and made him drink more. I therefore kept my mouth closed, but when he emptied his second glass as precipitately as the first I decided to leave immediately, fearing that his drinking would very soon get completely out of control.

Henry, however, seemed to sense what was going through my mind, for he desisted from pouring wine down himself as if it were water, and instead rose from his chair, bowed slightly to me and asked: "May I have the pleasure of the next dance?" Pleased that he seemed to have seen reason, I nodded, whereupon he took my hand and drew me from the table across to the dance floor. Here he held me close against him and danced with me as he had never done before. He whirled me around with such strength and speed that the dancing was a delight, and as the music changed to a calmer tempo he too elegantly moved into a slower mode, so that we remained dancing on the spot, pressed closely against each other. This gave me the opportunity to observe the other dancers, who were swirling all around us in time to the musicians' playing.

Suddenly my eye fell on someone dancing close to me: although his back was turned towards me I recognised him immediately as my former travelling companion Christian Bach.

Shocked, I felt like breaking off the dance and escaping from the dance floor, but then I thought better of it and continued dancing, since I was curious about Christian's partner and wanted to have a closer look at her. I had no idea if the young lady was Christian's fiancée or not, but judging from the way she was pressed up close against him and he was holding her in his arms, they could not be two complete strangers who had just happened to meet. Christian's partner was attractive to look at and of medium height.

She had dark brown eyes, shoulder-length black hair and red, sensual lips which, when she parted them to smile, revealed two rows of perfect white teeth. The whole of the young lady's posture was one of grace, and she was dressed in clothes which were modern without being extravagant. The only feature which detracted from her good looks was a conspicuously large goitre, which she attempted to conceal behind a wide necklace. In spite of this, I found her beautiful and was just beginning to feel jealous of her when the two of them spun round in their dance and Christian suddenly and unexpectedly caught sight of me.

For a moment he looked astonished and perplexed, but he soon regained his composure, and gave me a nod and smile of recognition. I replied with a forced smile, whereupon Christian danced across in my direction and called out: "How nice that you could come, Idilia!"

Henry, his attention thereby drawn to Christian, asked me how it was that I knew the German, to which I answered that I had made his acquaintance on the steamship. Thereupon Henry stopped dancing, grasped my hand and led me away from the dance floor. When we had reached our table he submitted me to a thorough cross-examination, wanting to know everything about my acquaintance with Christian. I endeavoured to portray it as innocently as was possible, and kept quiet about how painful it was to me to see him with the young lady. While Henry kept incessantly on and on at me, I could see that Christian and his partner had also stopped dancing, and were making their way over to us. When they reached us he greeted us both briefly, and then turned to Henry and said: "You must be Idilia's Henry?" Henry replied with an ill-humoured: "I was not aware that we were acquainted, sir".

Christian said that I had told him about him, which occasioned Henry to give me a withering look. In an attempt to reduce the tension, I asked the black-haired young lady at Christian's side who she was. Although I had asked in a friendly tone her reply was far from cordial, for she retorted, brusquely, "And who, I might ask, are you?" Taken aback by her abrupt reaction I realised that there was no point trying to pursue a conversation with her, so I took Henry by the arm and said, in a demonstratively affectionate tone, "Come on Henry, it's time for us to go home".

Thereupon Christian, who took my behaviour as being directed towards him, turned to face Henry, and in a derisive tone recommended him to buy ear plugs because of my loud snoring. With this suggestion the young lady and Henry both grimaced in the belief that we had committed some unbecoming trespass – only he and I knew that nothing had taken place between us.

In the desire to pay back Christian's companion for her unfriendliness and Christian for his indiscretion I asked her if he also pulled the blanket off her every night, and when the young lady stared at me, quite thunderstruck, I added with relish that Christian had in fact, on every night we had spent together, tugged the blanket off me and wrapped himself in it. This sally hit home, and Henry too looked shocked, while Christian stared at the ground with an embarrassed look on his face.

Feeling certain that my words would have serious consequences for all four of us, I ironically wished my interlocutors "A pleasant evening" and strode quickly away. Henry was immediately at my heels, and as he walked along behind me he tried to interrogate me about the exact nature of my relationship with "that German fellow". Disappointed at the turn events had taken I had no desire to answer any questions, but stormed onwards along the main street with my mouth tightly shut, and headed for the town gate.

I left the town with Henry at my side, and we started walking back in the late afternoon sun towards Niederlahnstein. As we walked Henry made several attempts to coax out of me an answer as to whether I had

had an affair with Christian or not. At length, worn down by Henry's persistent questioning, I gave up my resistance and explained to him that he had been the first man in my life and that that was still the case. I consciously couched my answer in vague words, but they nevertheless seemed to satisfy him completely, for he hugged me, gave me a pat on the cheek, and then left me in peace.

I on the other hand was far from pleased with the whole situation, partly because I had the feeling that after my performance in Oberlahnstein it would be impossible for me ever to have any further contact with Christian, and partly because here I was together with Henry, despite the fact that I had regarded myself as having finished with him a long time ago. When I asked him, as if in passing, how he envisaged spending the rest of his time in Germany, he answered that he had no intention of remaining in the country and would be returning to England on that very Sunday evening – and moreover, intended to take me with him.

Before I could raise any objection, he promised that, in compensation for interrupting my Rhineland holiday, he would treat me to a much finer one in London. He tried to tempt me with talk of art galleries, museums and restaurants, knowing full well that all I knew of London was what I had experienced while passing through, and that I longed to get to know the city properly. Although I had sworn to myself under no circumstances to let Henry talk me into anything at all, I felt that this was exactly what I was now allowing to happen. Noticing how uncertain I had become, he crowned his campaign of persuasion by holding out to me the prospect of a visit to the royal palace. That, he said complacently, surely outdid the old ruined castles along the Rhine, and I was obliged to concur. His promises and fine words made me compliant, and at length I half-heartedly declared myself prepared to accompany him back to England, although I asked to be given until Sunday afternoon to make up my mind definitively.

With the admonition not to wait too long in giving him my decision, Henry granted me this period of consideration. I could tell from his self-assured bearing that he was convinced that I would choose to go with him to England, although I myself was not at all so sure, since I had not yet put the matter to my parents, and what was more I could not get Christian Bach out of my thoughts. I was very much afraid that by departing prematurely from Germany I might be making a serious mistake which I would subsequently never be able to rectify. Indeed I was to a very great degree inwardly occupied by my relationship with Christian.

I wondered why he had ever invited me to the summer festival in Oberlahnstein at all, when he was connected with another girl from that town. Must he not surely have understood that if he attended the festival in my company he would risk her seeing us together? Or perhaps, it suddenly occurred to me, they were no longer betrothed and she was now simply a good friend of his, from whom he had no need to hide me? This explanation would also accommodate what Christian had told me before, namely that he was no longer engaged, I thought, and felt my hopes rise again. They immediately afterwards sank again, however, when I recalled how hostile the girl had been in her reaction to me, and how chivalrously Christian had treated her. I wanted very much to know why, and was determined to find out by Sunday at the latest. Sunday, I resolved, was to be the watershed for my future life, the day when it would be decided which course I was to take from here.

10

FATIGUED FROM our long walk to the Lahn, Henry and I sat down under a shady tree. Emboldened at the thought that he might soon be reunited with me Henry ventured to kiss me. As he did so he pushed me backwards onto the grass and, lying half over me, began tearing at my blouse. I defended myself vigorously, and after a moment he left me alone. I felt outraged at his impudent attack and I let him know in hard words what I thought of his behaviour, and gave him to understand that I would certainly not accompany him to England should he once more have the audacity to molest me in such a manner. He begged me to forgive him and sought to excuse his lack of restraint by pleading the long time that had lapsed since the last time we had known each other as man and woman. In this respect, I retorted, I was not at all moved to pity, since he had spent the time in question with his mistress. When Henry thereupon had the insolence to reply that he had only been unfaithful to me because I had shown no concern for him and had preferred your company, Gwen, to his, I had had enough of him; I rose from the grass and ran off, towards the river bank.

The sun was just going down as I reached the ferry house on the shore of the river. It was one of those sombre sunsets, when it seems as if the sun is sinking into obscurity for the rest of eternity. In this dusky light I stepped into the boat of the ferryman Anton Douqué, and asked him to row me over the river to Niederlahnstein. He had scarcely started pulling at the oars when we heard a loud whistle from behind us, and on turning round to see who had whistled like that we saw Henry, who was standing on the shore and waving his arms to indicate that he wanted us to take him with us. I had no desire to have him with us in the ferry boat, and I shook my head to communicate this to the friendly ferryman. He took my part, and continued rowing towards Niederlahnstein, paying no further heed to Henry who stood shouting and swearing on the shore.

When, twenty minutes later, I reached our inn, my family was sitting in the garden listening to Father, who was reading aloud from Lord Byron's "Childe Harold". To Mother's mistrustful question as to where Henry had got to I replied that I had no idea, but was sure that he would turn up before very long. Before she could subject me to any further questioning I left the garden and went up to my room, where I threw myself, fully dressed, onto the bed and, exhausted by all that I had been through during the day, immediately fell into a deep slumber.

I do not know for how long I had slept, but when I was woken by shouting from the ground floor I saw that it had grown dark. I lit a candle and heard the thud of heavy footsteps on the stairs. A moment later the door to my room was flung open from the outside and in came Henry, clearly in a state of agitation. Before I could enquire of him what the cause of his being so worked up was he told me, the words pouring out in a rush of indignation, that the young German we had encountered at the festival in Oberlahnstein had had the insolence to come to our inn and ask for me.

On hearing this I immediately arose in order to go to see Christian, but Henry pushed me back onto the bed and informed me in a sneering tone that I need not take the trouble, since he, Henry, had already thrown him out with his own hands. I was scandalised at this news, shook myself free from Henry and leapt towards the door, but he held me back, grasping my hips and thrusting me back onto the bed. He then locked the door from the inside, sat down in an armchair and gave every sign of remaining in the room with me. He had hereby once and for all spoiled any chance he might have had of regaining my affection, and I told him that I would definitely not be accompanying him back to England. To this however he reacted by giving a loud laugh, and said that my parents had already assented to my going with him. This I could not believe, and wanted to hear them say so with my own ears. Expecting that Henry would soon give up guarding me and that I would thus be able to go and talk to my family, I lay, completely motionless, on the bed, staring at the ceiling and ignoring Henry completely.

I had spent approximately ten minutes in this fashion when, from the open window, I heard a scraping noise, which had attracted Henry's attention too. Suddenly Christian appeared at the window, standing on a ladder, and called out to me that he absolutely needed to speak to me. When Henry saw who it was he crossed the room to the window and tried to prevent him from entering the room, shouting at him: "Have you taken leave of all your senses?"

A tumult arose at the window, and just as I got to my feet to go and assist Christian he pushed Henry aside and dived headlong into the room. Before Christian had time to clamber to his feet Henry cast himself over him and began belabouring him with kicks and blows, while at the same time hurling the vilest insults at him. Christian managed to regain his feet, and defended himself as best he could against his raging aggressor. I threw myself at Henry and, holding tightly to his back, endeavoured to make him stop – which in fact, after a deal of pushing, pulling and screaming I succeeded in doing.

Christian then told me that he had made several attempts to get to meet me in the public bar of the inn, but that Henry and my mother had denied him access. Seeing no other expedient he had climbed up to my window. He said that the reason for his late visit was that he wished to apologise to me for his unbecoming behaviour that afternoon. I accepted his apology quite calmly, and gave no outward sign to betray how inwardly glad it had made me, albeit I felt that in entering my room by the window he had gone a little too far.

Christian, who had no way of knowing what my thoughts were, was on the point of taking his leave of me when I suddenly remembered his travelling bag, which Mary had looked after on the ship and I had kept in safe-keeping for him. I gave Christian the bag, and he was visibly pleased at seeing it again. After he had opened it and made sure that his money and all his important papers were still in it, he thanked me and, shaking my hand, bade me farewell. I unlocked the door to allow Christian to leave; after nodding quickly to Henry, who however remained stony-faced and obstinately refused to return the greeting, he left the room with his shirt tails fluttering.

Scarcely had Christian left the room before my mother appeared in the doorway, expressing her displeasure at his presence in the building. When Henry, too, started complaining I told the two of them to go to the devil and stormed out of the room, burning with anger. I ran down the stairs and out of the inn, hoping that I would be able to catch up with Christian. I drew level with him not far from the inn, and apologised for Henry's attacks. Christian answered me with a smile, saying that it was his own fault because he had interfered too much in my life and the life of my family. In the same breath he promised that henceforth he would bother us no more, and wished me good fortune in my future life.

Before he could move away I restrained him by the sleeve and asked: "And what about your fiancée?", to which he responded: "We are not engaged any more". I continued my questioning, enquiring: "Is that really the truth?", and he nodded affirmatively. "Why?" I then asked, to which he replied, "Because we simply don't suit each other". Hereupon he freed himself from my grip and before I could move to hold him back he disappeared in the darkness along the river bank.

Convinced that I had seen Christian for the last time I returned, dejectedly, to the inn, where I was obliged to listen to a fierce scolding from my mother. She called me a hussy and a trollop for having received a visit from Christian, and threatened to cast me out of our family if I

190

did not come to my senses and go back to Henry. My distress at Christian's hasty farewell had robbed me of the strength to resist, with the result that I promised my mother that I would obey her. She instructed me to go to Henry and apologise to him for my childish behaviour. I did as she had told me and went up to his room where, sitting in an armchair, he graciously accepted my apology. Henry told me clearly that as of now he considered us once more to be engaged; he demanded that I should spend the night in his room, and also share the bed with him again. Since I was very downcast at parting from Christian and feeling too weak to rebel against Henry, I yielded to his will, and collected my effects and moved into his room.

Later on, while he sat drinking in the lounge together with my parents and other patrons of the inn, I sat at the writing table in the bedroom and, as I do every night, wrote up my diary.

Sunday, 15th June 1851
I had already gone to sleep when, towards midnight, Henry came into the bed and woke me with his kisses. As I pushed him away, disgusted at the heavy smell of alcohol on his breath, he made it unmistakably clear that he at long last wanted from me what I had refused him for weeks; he hurled himself over me and tried to take me with force. I defended myself desperately, and at length Henry gave up his aggression and left me in peace. Perspiring and strug-

gling to regain our breath we lay side by side in the bed; after we had recovered somewhat Henry turned to face me and, breaking the silence, asked: "Be honest with me Idilia – did you sleep with that German?"

Henry's question caught me unawares, and for a moment I did not know how to respond. However, I rapidly pulled myself together, and said that I had not. Once more the room was silent, but after a short while the quiet was again broken, as Henry asked me, his voice grown husky: "Do you love him?"

The deathly silence which succeeded his question provided him with the answer.

The following morning my family and I attended the morning service at the chapel of St Barbara, which was only a little way along the street from our inn. Henry did not accompany us; he was still sleeping heavily when we left. In the church my parents and brother and sister sat in one of the front pews, while I took a seat a few rows further back and to one side. I prayed fervently to God that he might forgive me for my pride, and give Christian back to me.

The officiating priest was just reeling off a prayer when the church door creaked to announce that it was being opened from the outside. I turned around, and to my great surprise I saw Christian, who was crossing himself and, on catching sight of me, came straight in my direction. Thrown off balance by his completely unexpected appearance, and by the speed with which my wish had been granted, I span back to face the altar. As I did so I saw my mother, who had turned around and was directing her stern stare in my direction. A moment later I heard a hissing behind me and turned round to see Christian, kneeling down in the row behind me. He whispered to me: "I forgot to give you this yesterday evening", and produced the ring which he had given me in Bonn and I had given back to him in Coblenz. He held out the ring towards me with a smile, and after giving him a searching look in order to ascertain what his intentions were, I took the ring and said to him in a whisper: "The next time you see me wearing the ring I'll be free. Wait for me at sunset by the ferry house on the Lahn".

Christian promised that he would be there, and smiled. When the other church-goers, disturbed by our whispering, began hissing at us to be quiet and casting annoyed looks in our direction, Christian rose from his pew, gave me a nod of farewell and hurriedly left the house of worship. Filled with gratitude that God had heard my plea and brought me back together with Christian, I immediately sent a prayer heavenwards.

After the service my mother asked me what Christian had wanted in the church; to assuage her suspicions I said that he had simply wanted my address in Edinburgh. My mother reacted by advising me to forget the German as quickly as possible and to devote myself solely to my betrothed, Henry, who, she informed me in reproachful tones, had complained to her that I had been neglecting him. I found this the height of hypocrisy on Henry's part, but took good care to conceal how I felt, and in order to forestall any more arguments I lied to her, saying that I would pay more attention to Henry in the future. My words seemed to satisfy her, and concord between us ostensibly restored, we returned to the inn.

When we got back Henry was up, and we ate breakfast in his company in the lounge. He was in an ill temper, and complained peevishly about first one thing and then the other, which led to a most cheerless mood developing at our table. My father endeavoured to cheer my brother and sister and myself up with joking, but Mother, who really has no sense of humour, told him gruffly to stop playing the fool. This meant that the tense atmosphere at table became even tenser, but fortunately relief came in the form of the blowing of a horn outside, shortly after which two postillions entered the lounge – the day before Father had ordered two diligences at the Turn und Taxische Postexpedition which were to take us to Bad Ems, and the postillions had come in to inform us that they were ready to depart. The two men, one short and fat and the other long and thin, were like two saviours for my brother and sister and me, since we were now finally able to leave the breakfast table and go out into the fresh air.

Outside the entrance to the inn there stood two diligences, harnessed in front of which were four fine white horses. Once Father had given the postillions the necessary directions, our baggage was stowed aboard, we took our places, and at about 10 am we left the town of Niederlahnstein. I sat together with Mary and Henry in the front carriage, and my brother George sat with our parents in the rear diligence. The road we were travelling along was in poor condition; it followed the Lahn, and owing to its proximity to the river at several places it lay under water. The seats in the diligence were hard, and the road was so uneven that we were given a very thorough shaking. This did not however prevent Henry from grasping my hand and, saying "So, now we are betrothed again", slipping onto my finger the engagement ring I had given back to him before I left Edinburgh.

I was repelled by the unromantic way in which he had foisted the ring onto me, and felt like nothing more than flinging the ring at Henry's feet, but I thought better of it and left the ring on my finger in order to avoid a scene, although I had already made up my mind definitively to break off my engagement with Henry. He was completely unsuspecting of my decision, and in his belief that I once more belonged to him began taking liberties with me. Without showing the least consideration towards my sister, who sat looking contemptuously at him, he fumbled at my blouse and made lewd remarks, swigging brandy all the while out of a hip-flask. His behaviour was, to put it mildly, disgraceful, and the further we travelled the greater became his degree of drunkenness and vulgarity. Although I made several attempts to get the postillion to stop the diligence, he just kept on driving; it was only when Henry roared at him to halt so that he could empty his bladder that he finally brought the diligence to a standstill. While he stood, without any shame, next to the coach and passed water, Mary and I fled to the other diligence and, citing Henry's unbearable behaviour, tried to persuade them to turn around and return to Niederlahnstein. My father, revolted at Henry's disgraceful manners, was in favour of doing as we wished, but my mother shouted at him that turning round was quite out of the question, and that we must continue our journey as we had planned. Since my father once more was unable to prevail against the will of my mother, Mary and I had no choice but to grit our teeth, climb back up into our diligence, and resume our journey in the company of the drunken Henry.

The alcohol soon had the effect of making him tired, so the rest of the journey, with the exception of the occasional cynical comment which he directed at me, was relatively problem-free – although what with the shaking and swaying of the coach it was nonetheless arduous enough. Despite the discomfort Henry fell asleep, for which my sister and I were very grateful, since at home in Scotland we had on one or two occasions experienced him so drunk that we feared for our lives.

After travelling about 15 miles through delightful countryside we arrived in glorious sunshine, at about midday, at Bad Ems, which is situated in a steep gorge of the Lahn valley. On the left bank of the river are the world-famous Emser springs, or "Emser Quellen"; there is an imposing bath-house with four towers, fine buildings housing assembly rooms, and three marble drinking fountains in the classical style from which warm, bubbling medicinal water flows.

We alighted from our conveyances with stiff, aching limbs, and had a good stretch until we felt comfortable again. Father instructed the postillions to wait for us, whereupon we took our first walk through the attractive spa, which was crowded with visitors from every imaginable country.

It was conspicuous to us that there were a great many Britons there, either as paying guests who had come to take the waters, or simple tourists such as ourselves. After a deal of walking around the resort we became hungry and thirsty, so we stopped at an elegant restaurant to enjoy the cool shade and refresh ourselves with food and drink. When we had sat and rested for long enough Father paid the bill and we continued our tour of the admirable resort. Since Henry had poured one or two glasses of wine too many down his throat during our meal he was drunk again, but he tried to save appearances and conceal the fact. However, his unsteady gait and the reddening of his face revealed rather clearly to us in what condition he was. Mary kept herself at a marked distance from him, and darted contemptuous glances at him from time to time.

We came to an impressive building in which a large number of neat young girls were employed filling the Bad Ems water into thousands of earthenware jars. As if by command they bent down and dipped ten jars at a time into the water, and then lifted them out, filled with water, and placed them on the ground beside themselves. This procedure was repeated until the hardworking maidens grew tired, when they were relieved by another team of bottling girls. We visitors tasted the water in tumblers and were unanimous in finding that it tasted much better than the water that was dispatched bottled in jars. Only Henry, who by now was even drunker, declared that he could taste no difference, and proclaimed this loudly for all to hear. He then made an attempt to take up with the smartly dressed bottling girls, but when they politely tried to fend him off, he grew angry and insulted them in English, using obscene language.

My father and I, feeling extremely embarrassed, tried to induce him to leave the building, and when this proved unsuccessful and Henry continued to disturb the girls in their work, one of their number ran out to fetch help. I tried to drag Henry away from the girls, and he responded by slapping me in the face so hard that my nose started bleeding.

I ran weeping out of the building, and at the door I unexpectedly bumped into Christian, whom I almost did not recognise since he was dressed in working clothes. He was just as astonished to see me as I was to see him, and after our feelings of surprise had subsided a little he wanted to help me see to my nose, being concerned at seeing it bleed. I waved his attentions aside, however, and said, as I wiped away the blood with a handkerchief, that I could take care of myself and that he should rather go in and throw the troublemaker out – although I omitted to mention that the troublemaker was Henry.

Christian thereupon entered the bottling house, from inside which I could hear Henry's shouting and the panic-stricken shrieking of the girls. As I tried to cast a look into the building Henry suddenly burst out of the door with a demented expression in his eyes, almost trampling me under foot.

When he saw me he halted for a moment, mumbled something which I could not make out, and then continued out into the park, where he was swallowed up by the crowds.

In the bottling house I could see Christian lying lifeless on the floor, surrounded by bottling girls and visitors who were looking after him. I was worried for him, and shoved my way through the ranks of people standing around him. I reached him just as he came round. He struggled to his feet, still looking rather dazed, but he brightened up when he saw me, and gave me a weak smile. I asked him what had happened, and learned that when Christian had tried to persuade Henry to leave the building, Henry had struck him to the ground. I started apologising to Christian, but he waved my words aside, and said that there was no need for me to apologise, since the whole thing was not as bad as all that. Indeed, he tried to see the positive side of the incident, and jokingly said that had it not been for Henry's scene, then we would certainly not have seen each other in Bad Ems. I had to agree with him on that point, and before we could talk any more about it my father and brother and sister came over to us, anxious to ask Christian how he was.

Only my mother remained standing at a distance, adopting a pose as if none of this episode had anything to do with her. Her attitude caused me to give her a reproachful stare, to which she reacted by turning on her heel and leaving the bottling house. Her reaction did not escape Christian, who gave me a pained smile, and then told me that he unfortunately had to return to his work, but that we would at all events be seeing each other that evening. I nodded in acknowledgement and then, still embarrassed at what had occurred, asked if the police would be calling Henry to account for his belligerent misdeed. Christian answered that he would endeavour to persuade the management of the spa not to raise a charge against Henry, which calmed my anxiety, although I was still feeling furious at Henry for his scandalous misconduct. As we were making our way out of the bottling house Christian said, in a conciliatory tone, that Henry had certainly already begun to regret the way he had behaved and was probably waiting for a suitable opportunity to apologise. I was not at all sure that this was the case, but I felt thankful that Christian was magnanimous enough to grant my former fiancé at least a final remnant of decency.

Christian accompanied me part of the way through the park, and as we parted at the assembly rooms I spontaneously embraced him, holding him tightly against me for a moment. He then went into the building, and I rejoined my father and brother and sister, who were sitting on a bench close by waiting for me. Mother and Henry were nowhere to be seen, and since Father was worried at the thought of what the two of them might get up to in the condition they were in, we immediately set off to look for them. George complained of a bad stomach ache, which was probably caused by the disagreeable episode of which Henry had made himself guilty. Mary, too, who was very pale in the face, seemed to be suffering as a result of the incident. Father was desperately trying to remain calm and composed, but it was not difficult to see that he in truth was feeling very tense and uneasy. As for myself, I had but one single wish: that we could conclude our visit to Bad Ems as soon as possible, so that I could then tell Henry to disappear from my life.

After having had to interrupt our search for Mother and Henry several times, owing to George's frequent need to visit the lavatory, we finally located them sitting in a café garden drinking coffee. When Mother caught sight of us her face twisted into a grimace, while Henry demonstratively looked off in another direction and acted as if we were not there. When Father anxiously asked Mother what her plans were for the rest of the afternoon she snapped back at him that she wanted us to leave her in peace. Her callous insolence annoyed me beyond all measure; with anger in my voice I asked her why she was being so hideous towards us, at the same time as she was being so pleasant towards Henry despite the fact that his behaviour was that of an idiot. She replied in a hateful tone that I should keep my impudent mouth shut and get out of her sight. This was a favour I really did feel like doing her, but when I saw Henry grinning derisively at me I decided that I would first give him something to take the grin off his face.

I walked up to the table, pulling the engagement ring off my finger as I approached. I stood at the table, and to Mother's and Henry's speechless astonishment dropped it into Henry's coffee cup, declaring at the same time that our betrothal was over and that I would never resume my connection with him. Before he had time to react I turned and left him, and made my way back over to my father and brother and sister. I explained to them that I wished to make my way back to Niederlahnstein on my own, on foot; they nodded their agreement and striding as quickly as I could I set off in the direction of the Lahn.

I heard my mother calling after me to come back straight away, but I paid no heed to her and pushed on towards the river. When I reached the bank I saw an elderly man sitting in his boat mending a fishing net; when I asked him if he could row me over to the other side he put aside his work in order to help me, and once I had alighted on the other shore he rowed back to the left bank of the Lahn while I began walking along the right bank, following a narrow tow-path in the direction of Niederlahnstein. I had chosen this route with care, since the last thing I wanted was for my mother and Henry to catch up with me in their diligence and force me to journey home with them. By walking along this riverside path I knew I was safe from them; the only cause I had for concern was whether I would be able to reach the ferry houses by sunset to keep my rendez-vous with Christian. Since I had a good 15 miles' walk ahead of me I kept up a rapid pace, and felt I had good hopes of arriving at our tryst in time.

11

THE SUN WAS shining hotly, and the air blowing off the Lahn grew warmer as I walked along, with my hands behind my back and my gaze directed either at the ground in front of me or at the surrounding countryside. All the features which go to compose a beautiful landscape were on view: among the wealth of vegetation along the river there were yellow water-lilies, dragonflies were flitting above the water, and bees were buzzing in and out of the harebells. It was a joy to walk in this valley, passing between low hills and woods, slopes decked with flowers and moss-covered cliffs. The colours of the bushes, rocks and the clear, smoothly flowing river blended and together with the blue sky which was reflected with its white clouds in the water combined to form a delightful whole. The wind made the trees sway, and the appearance of the water and sky changed constantly. The air was filled with the joyful singing of birds in the woods and meadows and the chirping of crickets in the tall grass. Here and there a stream came down from the heights between the mosses and ferns to merge its waters with the clear, green waters of the Lahn. After a while of rapid walking in the heat I grew very warm, and I longed to cool myself and wash off the perspiration caused by my exertions. Finding a place where the river was shallow I removed my clothes in the shelter of a bush, and stepped into the water. Having refreshed myself I lay in the sun on the shore to dry myself, and then dressed and strolled on my way again, musing to myself as I progressed along the path. Not a single other person was to be seen.

Although my ramble from Bad Ems to Niederlahnstein had passed through charming countryside I was happy when, before sunset, I reached the ferry buildings on the right-hand side of the river. Christian was already waiting there for me, sitting on a tree trunk and gazing out over the river, lost in thought. He was dressed in a beige-coloured tail coat, and beside him there was a basket covered with a red and blue checked tea towel. I called out his name and on seeing me he started up from the tree trunk and stared at me in surprise. When he had recovered himself some-what he came towards me and called out: "Idilia, where've you come from? I thought you'd be coming over with the

Lahn ferry boat". I answered with a shake of my head, and said "No, I came on foot".

"But surely not all the way from Bad Ems?" he asked, looking at me in disbelief. By now I had come up to Christian, and I gave an affirmative nod in answer to his question. He then asked me why I had come the way I had, and I said it was because of a family disagreement and explained briefly to him what had taken place in Bad Ems. He understood that I had decided to return to Niederlahnstein alone, and expressed his admiration for my courage. I then showed Christian that I was wearing the ring he had given me on my ring finger, indicating thus to him that I was henceforth free of Henry for good. Christian took me in his arms and kissed me. I returned his kiss and he became more ardent, kissing me with increasing passion. Between the kisses he declared how much he had missed me, and how happy he was that I had been able to come to him this evening. I whispered in Christian's ear that I was happy to be with him, and with my passion showed him how deeply felt these words were. We had fallen to our knees, still mouth on mouth, and were about to continue our kissing lying in the grass when the sound of someone clearing their throat close at hand made us jump up.

It was Anton, the ferryman, informing us that he was there; he made the friendly suggestion that we might be well advised to find a better place for our love than his ferry point. Blushing, we hastened to follow his well-intentioned advice and scrambled to our feet. Christian picked up his basket, took me by the arm and led me between the trees up the steep, wooded slope. Clinging to the top of this craggy incline was the ruined castle of Lahneck where, Christian revealed to me, he had planned that we would have our picnic. I greeted his plan enthusiastically; all my walking had left me hungry and thirsty, and the idea of a romantic dinner for two in the open air was a joy to my ears. We began climbing up to the old ruin, ascending a path on which unhewn stones had been laid to serve as steps, catching hold of bushes, roots and tufts of grass to keep our balance.

The mountain became steeper and steeper, and the path with its rough steps seemed to have no end. However, after about half an hour, we finally arrived at the summit, which was thickly covered with bushes and weeds. We stood on the threshhold to the ruin, with mosquitoes swarming around us, and looked at the thirteenth-century castle, which really was in an extremely dilapidated condition. Wherever we looked we saw tumbledown walls and ramshackle towers, with jackdaws' nests, empty window frames, and floors to which no stairs any longer ascended. I can attest that thistles flourish on mountains which are topped with ruined castles. Ivy entwined itself like jungle lianas around the remains of caved-in walls, and thousands of wild plants and flowers formed a lush, scented terrace.

The inside of the castle did not present a more cheerful aspect: the stonework was eroded and full of holes, the ceilings and roofs had collapsed and roots had cracked their way through the stones of the courtyard. Wild berry and briar bushes were growing out of the cellar vaults, which were thickly hung with cobwebs. There was one fine-looking tower which invited one to climb it, and Christian and I made the spontaneous decision that we would partake of our picnic up at the top of the tower, so that we could enjoy the Rhineland prospect afforded to us by this high vantage point as we ate.

Inside the dark walls of the tower a spiral wooden stairway led us up to the grass-covered platform at the top. When we looked over the parapet we had a breath-takingly wonderful view over the beautiful countryside which looked like a living relief map that had been rolled out beneath us. We walked round the circumference of the tower, and on the left, on the far side of the Rhine, we saw the fairy-tale castle of Stolzenfels. Straight in front of us steam-ships pounded northwards along the shimmering river, their funnels blowing out smoke as they sailed past the extensive vineyards. To our right we saw farms and small villages embedded amid pretty pastures, woodlands and open fields. Deep below us, when we looked over the edge of the steep cliff, we could see the river Lahn and the town of Niederlahnstein, and behind us were the heights of the Taunus mountains. We could hear the twittering and warbling of countless birds, a train in the distance, the ringing of bells and the lowing of cattle in the pastures.

When we had finished enjoying the captivating view Christian politely invited me to take a seat, and once we were both seated on the ground he removed the red and blue checked cloth from the basket, and spread it on the ground between us as a tablecloth. From the basket he took a bottle of wine, plates and cutlery, and bread, a piece of cheese and German sausage, "wurst". When Christian had finished setting our "table" and placed a small oil lamp on it he poured us each out a glass of wine, which shone blood-red in the glasses. We clinked our glasses together and each drank a mouthful; thereafter our meal could begin, and we ate with relish.

Since we had come to the ruin at sunset, night fell while we were at the top of the tower. Christian lit the oil lamp, and we continued eating in the warm glow it cast over us. We emptied our glasses and refilled them to the brim, and then at once drank from them. As we ate and drank we carried on in animated conversation about every kind of topic, from the state of the world to personal matters. For the first time Christian told me about Mathilde, also known as Tilly, his former fiancée. She was the daughter of a potter from the town of Braubach am Rhein, and last year she had fallen in love with an apprentice potter in her father's workshop. Christian told me that because of this the girl's strict father had thrown her out of the house, thus rendering her homeless. In her affliction she had remembered her childhood friend Christian, and been given shelter by him in Bad Ems. Not for love, but as a temporary measure to help Tilly and in order to ensure that people's tongues would not wag, he became betrothed to her. However, he was soon forced to realise that she no longer saw him as a friend who had helped her in her need, but as her future husband. When Christian understood this he wished to end their relationship, but she had then threatened to commit suicide if he did; and indeed, ever since then she had used this threat as a means of making sure that he did not leave her. Out of fear that she would carry out her threat Christian had not dared to terminate their connection; it was only meeting me, he averred, that had caused him to have serious thoughts about leaving her for good and taking the risk that she might end her own life.

I understood that Christian was caught in a difficult dilemma, although what I could not understand was that the girl should use such a method to attempt to bind Christian to herself. To my worried question as to whether he really had brought his engagement to her to an end he assured me that he had, although he expressed the concern he felt that Tilly might do away with herself. I said to him that most would-be suicides usually go no further than issuing their threats, and he sided with this position, adding that Tilly would probably outlive us both. I fervently hoped that this would not be the case; and in order to cheer ourselves up after this rather dispiriting conversation we once more clinked our glasses together and drank to a long life.

After we had drained our glasses in silence, Christian said: "It's a pity we didn't have the opportunity to dance with each other at the festival in Oberlahnstein, for I love dancing." I responded by saying that I was not a very good dancer, but this did not seem to worry him, for he said, paying no attention to what I had just said: "We can dance here, if you would like to". I objected that we had no music, but he answered with a smile: "That doesn't matter. We can imagine the music – for example, a slow waltz". On saying this he rose to his feet, and then took me by the hand and pulled me up from the ground. His slim fingers closed around my hand, and I felt rather clumsy as he lay his arm around my waist. Christian took a firmer hold of me and I slipped into his arms, and as he drew me nearer to him my clumsiness disappeared. He started humming a melody, to which we danced slowly on the spot. He bent down to me and placed his cheek against mine. I could sense his warm, pleasant smell in my nose. Our legs, and sometimes our stomachs, moved close against each other. We pressed our bodies together, and it felt so beautiful that I wished our dance would never end.

It was warm at the top of the tower. Far off in the east we saw flashes of lightning, and we could hear the rumbling of distant thunder. Two moths fluttered around our oil lamp, attracted by the flickering light. One of them singed its wings by flying too close to the flame; it flitted aimlessly back and forth for a while, before disappearing in the black hole leading to the spiral stairway. I withdrew my cheek from Christian's and looked up into his eyes; he bent down towards me and kissed me tenderly on the mouth. I willingly returned his kiss, and as I lay my arms around his neck we stopped dancing. Christian placed his left hand on my hip, while with his right he stroked my face and hair. We then lowered ourselves to the ground without interrupting our kiss, and as we swept aside the "tablecloth", with the remains of our meal and our used dishes on it, to make space the wine bottle tipped over and its dark red contents spilled out onto the ground like blood. We paid no heed to the spillage, as we lay in each other's arms at the top of the tower; and by the light of the moon and the oil lamp we surrendered ourselves to the demands of love.

Afterwards we lay naked on our soft bed, which was composed of Christian's and my clothes, and looked up at the sparkling stars in the night sky, tired but filled with happiness after our act of love. We remained lying there for a long time, enjoying the pleasure of being together. Christian told me an old legend which I found very gripping. It was about a young German squire, or *junker*, who every evening rode across the Lahn to visit his sweetheart at Lahneck castle, provided her veil was hanging from the parapet of the tower as a sign to him that the coast was clear and he could come. One night, however, the water level in the Lahn was so high that the squire had drowned, and since then, Christian told me, the ghost of the squire's sweetheart had come to stand on the tower and wave her veil, and would do so until doomsday.

Christian then revealed that we were now in that very same tower; I started to shiver, and although the night was very warm I suddenly felt cold. I quickly dressed, and Christian did the same. Since we did not wish to be late in arriving at the ferry houses and have to wake the ferryman in the middle of the night, we hurriedly gathered together our picnic things and put them in the basket, before descending the creaking wooden stairs by the light of the oil lamp.

On arriving back on ground level we walked around the dark ruin for a little while longer; we could hear the beating of bats' wings and perceived rustlings, squeaks and buzzes from every side. In isolated places such as this, in the dark of the night, one soon becomes suspicious, and although I was with Christian I felt uneasy, so I was happy when we finally located the way out and could begin our climb back down the mountain.

The forest was however even more sinister, since we could hear the terrible cries of screech owls, and saw, among the trees and bushes, large and small pairs of eyes which reflected the glow from Christian's lamp. I clung anxiously onto Christian, who tried to make me feel less afraid with calming words. After an eternity of stumbling in the darkness over roots, stones and tufts of grass we finally arrived at the ferry houses on the right bank. Here we were happy to discover that the friendly ferryman, Anton Douqué, was still up, and was sitting by his boat with an oil lamp, waiting for us. Our intention was for him to row me over the river to Niederlahnstein, while Christian would spend the night in one of the ferry houses and then walk into Oberlahnstein in the morning. He had told me that he was obliged to travel away on business for a day or two, but he promised that when he returned home he would visit me at the "Coblenzer Hof", where he assumed that I would be spending the rest of my holiday with my family. I was not certain of this, since I did not know whether Henry had already left or if he was still in Niederlahnstein.

The moment came when I had to say goodbye to Christian, and although I was soon going to see him again my heart was close to breaking. I would never have conceived that a man could arouse such strong feelings in me, and I felt unable to part from him. I held him tightly, kissed him and pressed myself against him, wanting never to let him go again. When the ferryman, who throughout had waited patiently for us, started to grumble, Christian carefully released himself from my grasp and said tenderly: "You have to go now, my beloved".

He walked with me to the ferry boat, his arm around my hip, and paid the ferryman for the crossing. We kissed a final time, a long, deeply heartfelt kiss, and told each other how much we loved each other. Thereafter I clambered into the boat, in the bows of which an oil lamp was burning, and took a seat in the stern. As the ferryman rowed out into the river I looked back towards Christian, who stood on the shore, waving to me and smiling. I waved back, and kept on waving until I could see him no more in the darkness that engulfed the shore. At this moment I was overtaken by the terrible feeling that I would never see Christian again; suddenly the tears sprang to my eyes, and I started to weep. I was still weeping when the boat reached the left bank of the Lahn.

Anton consoled me, and after I had calmed myself somewhat I thanked the ferryman for the crossing and got out of the boat. I then walked in the dark along the bank of the Lahn, and five minutes later reached the inn. To my great disappointment all the lights in the inn were extinguished, and what was more, the door was locked. After I had hammered on the door with my fists a few times the door was opened by the sleepy landlord, who was holding an oil lamp in his hand, and was dressed in a long nightgown with a night-cap on his head. He let me in, mumbling something incomprehensible. I thanked him, saying "Dankeschön", and then tiptoed up the stairs so as not to wake anybody. However, on the first floor I was intercepted by my mother, who had been waiting for me in the dark. She jumped out at me suddenly, almost scaring me to death. She would certainly not have minded if I had fallen down dead; she was furious at me for coming home so late, and scolded me fiercely because Henry, owing to what she called my childish behaviour in Bad Ems, had left to return home. She threatened to punish me severely for my disobedience, but at that moment I couldn't care less, since I was inwardly overjoyed at learning that Henry had finally given me up and had decided to travel back home without me. I made sure, however, that I did not let my joy show, and made a pretence of having been chastened by Mother's hard words. With feigned submissiveness I asked for permission to go to my room, and with an impatient wave of her hand she gave me to understand that I should go.

Just as I was opening the door to my room Mother called after me that tomorrow we would be returning to Coblenz, so I could put any other plans out of my mind. I answered pertly that she had no need to worry about me, and said nothing to reveal that I had already made up my mind to return to Lahneck castle very early in the morning; I had not made any drawings of the ruin, and was set on making up for this so that I should have a remembrance of my night at the top of the tower with Christian. After giving my mother a "Good night, sleep well" which she sullenly returned, I entered the room and closed the door behind me. My brother and sister lay deep in slumber; I myself, despite its having been a very eventful day, was not at all tired, so I lit an oil lamp and sat down at the writing table to write my diary.

Monday, 16th June 1851
I was still writing when, through the east-facing window, I saw the red glow heralding sunrise. As the sun rises from behind the Taunus mountains I am writing these lines to conclude my first diary. I shall begin on a second volume today, dear Gwen, once I have been able to purchase a new book for the purpose, since I have not yet made such a provision.

The idea occurs to me to ask Mary to give me hers: it is a small volume; she has in any case not written a single line in it and will probably not do so.

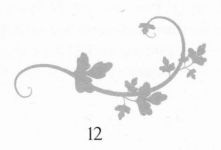

12

GOD IN HEAVEN, what is it that has happened? Am I dreaming or is this real? When I came to Lahneck, I ran swiftly up the creaking, rickety old wooden stairs inside the ruined tower, and just as I reached the top I heard a terrible crashing and clattering, which sent shivers of dread deep into my soul. I held my breath and closed my eyes and listened for a moment; and then I turned round and looked down, and what a sight confronted my eyes! The stairway had collapsed behind me. I stood for a while as if petrified, unable to think, almost unconscious, all my emotions numbed. It was as if I was no longer alive. Alas, if only that were the case!

I soon came round from this state, back to an existence and a situation which one can unequivocally call horrendous. I can discover no way of getting down. The walls are high, and there are but very few, widely separated projecting places. No pole, no rope, no help anywhere in sight.

Oh my lover! Oh Father, oh Mother! George and my dear sister Mary! How you will search for me, how you will shout my name, and wail in despair! And all the while I shall be here, at the top of this lonely, abandoned, desolate tower, without any means of giving you a sign that I am here, alive.

The livelong day I have shouted and yelled, but nobody has heard me. I do not think that my voice is strong enough to carry down from this height. I do not dare to approach the edge of the opening where the stairs crashed down, for fear that I might tumble down. In the first moment of my fear I hastened to the opening, but the horrific depth with its impenetrable blackness made me feel so dizzy that I stumbled back from the hole, half unconscious.

I have written messages on all the pages of my sketchbook and thrown them down, one by one. I saw that some of them floated away over the trees, while others drifted straight down into the water. Alas! If only I had been able to fly down from the tower with them! But no, the high wall of the parapet keeps me enclosed.

I then tried, in vain, to clamber up onto the parapet, but I am not strong enough. For as long as I could wave my arms I waved with my handkerchief in all directions. Nothing was of any effect, not a single soul noticed me. And yet I know, Father, Mother, George, Mary, that you are looking for me with anguish in your hearts, that you have set others to help you search for me. Will no-one think of coming to this tower? Not even Christian? Oh, come my beloved, come and rescue me!

Oh dear God above! I have been crying all day long, and now night is coming on. It is growing cold, and I am shivering. I can hear the trees below, rustling in the evening breeze, and above me the birds of the night are rising into the sky with heavy beats of their wings.

Tuesday, 17th June 1851
Curled up in a corner, bitterly weeping and sobbing, I fell asleep. I awoke very early, as day was about to break. I am freezing cold, and so hungry! My tongue is sticking to the roof of my mouth. Father of all creation, will You not send me deliverance? Am I really to be lost? My parents, brother and sister, friend, lover, can it be that no intuitive idea leads you to this spot? If one of you were to come to this place you would find me, my heart would guide you,

my poor heart which is choking with fear, pain, hunger, thirst and my own tears.

Once more I have shouted, waved, made every possible effort. My hands, my knees, my whole body are aching. My eyes and lips are burning, and my ears are filled with a dreadful buzzing. God, dear God, is no help to be granted me?

A hundred times I thought I heard people's voices. I seemed to hear Mother's voice quite clearly, calling my name. Mother, your poor child, your Idilia! Does no dark prompting of your soul impel you to this place? Mary, George, surely you must hear me! Listen, listen! Your sister is calling, your poor, despairing sister! In vain, all in vain!

In my deadly fear I have started to scratch loose stones out of the mortar with my fingernails, in order to pile them up and make steps. My fingers bled terribly, and once, when in pain I lifted my fingers to my mouth and felt and tasted the warm liquid, I felt like tearing myself apart so that I should have blood to drink. My blood did me good! Dear God, it is all I have taken for the past forty eight hours. I have already chewed the straw of my hat. But however much I long for food, the appallingness of my situation soon makes me forget all bodily needs.

All day long I piled up the stones I had managed to free from the mortar. Finally, towards sunset, the heap seemed to me to be high enough for me to reach the top of the parapet, which was previously reached by means of a few wooden steps, the rotting remains of which are lying around up here. I climbed up my heap of stones. The country lay spread out beneath me. How calm and peaceful it all was! In all the villages I could see smoke rising from the chimneys, and there was a steam-ship sailing on the Rhine. I waved energetically with my handkerchief, and thought I saw someone waving back at me! The happy people down there must have believed that I was waving a cloth in joyful greeting. Alas, they did not suspect how much it was a sign of distress and despair! For them the music of the band was playing on the afterdeck, for them the shores, the hotel, the arms of their loved-ones were waving. And what waves at me? Death, death is waving at me from every corner of this horrible ruin. And what kind of death? Father, Mother, George, Mary, Christian my beloved, do you want me to die in such a gruesome, gruesome way?

Wednesday, 18th June 1851

Am I still alive? It feels to me as if I have been up here for all eternity; my tongue is stuck against the top of my mouth; I am unable to call out any more. My clothes are in tatters, my hair is in disarray; I think I have become deaf, I hear nothing, it is as if the whole world were deserted.

Yesterday two swifts flew up and came to rest on the edge of the parapet. It was the final piece of happiness to be granted me, a greeting from the world, from life. When they flew off I watched them as long as I could, and thought that they must surely fly straight to my loved-ones to bring them news of my distress.

Thursday, 19th June 1851

This is, I think, the fourth day, the fourth infernal eternity. Yesterday it seemed I could hear once more. Everything was horrendously dead and quiet, it was as if I was in the grave, unable to feel, with no thoughts, no meaning. Suddenly I heard my name, as if it was being called far away, from our house in Edinburgh. I struggled to my feet and again climbed up on the heap of stones I made. I could not see! There was a veil before my eyes. I started swaying, and this caused the stones to slip, and I fell to the ground.

How long I lay, made unconscious by the fall, I do not know. All I know is that there is no hope for me. My death is certain. Once more I wish to pray for my soul's salvation, and for you my beloved, my father, my mother, George, Mary and Gwen. Then I will see if I still have strength enough to drag myself to the dark opening and throw myself down. Why oh why did I not do so straight away?

"Father in heaven, have mercy on my soul".

EPILOGUE

In 1860, after Idilia Dubb's 25-year-old brother George and her mother Elizabeth, at a police station in Coblenz, had confirmed that the items found in the tower at Lahneck Castle were those of the missing girl, their sister and daughter respectively, the two mourners travelled by steam-ship, in the company of two officials of the Prussian police, to the grand duchy of Hessen/Nassau.

The authorities in Oberlahnstein had kept the mortal remains of Idilia Dubb in the town hall, and that evening in this building, her mother and brother were received by the mayor of the town, Josef Müller, flanked by the chief clerk of the town hall, Georg Schultes, and the town's priest, Jakob Mohr. Once the men had expressed their condolences to the Dubbs the party progressed to a vault of the building, where the Dubbs were shown the simple wooden coffin in which Idilia's bones lay. Upset at being confronted with the remains of her daughter, the girl's mother was shaken by an attack of weeping, and she broke down by the side of the coffin. She soon recovered her composure, but was so gripped by sorrow that she was unable to answer the mayor's question as to what she wished to be done with Idilia's mortal remains – if they were to be transported to Scotland or if they were to be committed to German soil. Mother and son then left the town hall and betook themselves to the Hotel Lahneck, where they were to stay during the time they were to spend in the town.

On their way to the hotel Elizabeth Dubb was over-taken by a fainting fit, and was taken by her son and the clerk to the house of three elderly sisters who worked as nurses in Oberlahnstein. Mrs Dubb spent the night and the following day in their care, while her son stayed as planned at the hotel.

In the light of what Idilia had written in her diary George wished to get in touch with Christian Bach, but nobody in the town knew of his whereabouts. George Dubb was on the verge of abandoning his search when he heard from the priest, Jakob Mohr, who was to read the service for Idilia, that Christian Bach's former fiancée Tilly was living in the neighbouring town of Braubach.

In the hope that she would be able to help him track

Christian down George Dubb took the stagecoach to that town, where he learned in the pottery from Tilly's father that his daughter was living at "Burg Braubach", which was situated close by. This imposing fortress, built on the top of a high mountain, served as the electorate's prison. A commanding officer was in charge of a garrison of disabled soldiers, who lived there with their wives and children. George Dubb located the former fiancée of Christian Bach; she was married to one of the soldiers of the garrison and had four children.

Tilly, who had grown stout and was in ill health, was suspicious of George Dubb's intentions, and claimed not to know what had become of the man she was formerly betrothed to. However, when he gave her a handful of coins her tongue loosened, and she explained that Christian Bach lived a secluded life in one of the neighbouring villages. She did not want to reveal which village it was, and even when George Dubb offered her more money she would not soften her resolve. She did however reveal that after Idilia's disappearance he had been in shock for a considerable length of time – and had even tried to take his own life. George Dubb enquired after further details, and Tilly explained that Christian, five days after Idilia's disappearance, had turned up at the home of his former fiancée, covered in blood and with his clothes all torn; on being admitted to the house he had fallen into a coma-like deep sleep, which lasted for a full week. At the end of this time Christian came round and then, without saying a word, left Tilly's house. Tilly was firmly convinced that he had wounded himself when trying to commit suicide by hanging, and in proof she produced the length of cord he had had in his hand when he appeared at her door.

When George Dubb saw the cord, which was about one yard long and frayed at one end, he started in dismay, for he recognised that what he was looking at was not in fact a piece of cord, but a twisted piece of the dress Idilia had been wearing at the time of her disappearance in the summer of 1851. Remains of the dress had been found in the tower and were among the effects which George and his mother had received from the police in Coblenz. He at once could see that the piece of twisted cloth in Tilly's possession was identical to the remnant of material which had been found in the ruined castle of Lahneck and which he had on his person. He dismissed Tilly's theory that Christian Bach had tried to kill himself, believing instead that Christian, in the course of his search for Idilia, had discovered the length of cloth at the tower, and injured himself in his endeavour to recover it.

Tilly averred that Christian had never told her what had happened. George Dubb renewed his request to her to give him Bach's address so that he could talk to him himself. Tilly persisted in her refusal to reveal the location of Christian's abode, although she did promise George Dubb that she would ensure that Christian got to know of the presence in Oberlahnstein of Idilia's mother and brother.

On that same day the reverend Jakob Mohr held a memorial service for Idilia Dubb in the Church of St Martin in Oberlahnstein. The service was attended by both her brother George and her mother, who had by now recovered from her nervous breakdown. Following the service they remained in the church and prayed in silence, and as they did so a man dressed in black who walked with the aid of a stick entered the church. He crossed the nave, limping with his left leg, and when he arrived at Idilia's coffin he threw himself over it, sobbing with grief. At first Mrs and George Dubb were unable to recognise this man whose sorrow was so heart-rending, but after a moment they realised that it was Christian Bach, whose hair, once dark brown, was now completely grey.

He spent a long time clasping the coffin and weeping over it, and then relinquished his hold of it and walked over to George and Elizabeth Dubb. In a voice choked with tears he offered them his condolences, and told them how much he had loved Idilia. Before the Dubbs could think of anything to say in return he moved away and began limping towards the door. Since George had some questions he wished to ask him he ran after Christian, catching up with him outside, at the church gate. Dubb thanked him for his expression of sympathy, and then showed him the twisted piece of cloth from Idilia's dress, and wanted to know what had happened. After an initial refusal Christian, under the pressure of George Dubb's questioning, gave up his resistance and began to relate his story.

He told George that he had learned of Idilia's disappearance on returning from a short business trip on 19th June 1851. In the course of his desperate search for her he passed the ruined castle of Lahneck, where he noticed a flock of crows which kept flying around one of the towers, occasionally landing on it. Christian recognised it as the tower where he and Idilia had spent their last night together; alarmed by the unrelenting way in which the crows stayed close to the tower, and filled with foreboding, he climbed up to the ruin. He looked in at the base of the tower, and discovered that the spiral wooden staircase had collapsed; there was nothing left of it but a pile of broken planks.

With the courage born of despair and at great peril to his own life Christian Bach then climbed up the wooden wreckage which was piled up inside the tower. Wounded by splinters and nails, and with his clothes torn to rags, he finally succeeded in reaching the top of the collapsed staircase. From this position he could see above him the hole leading up to the platform at the top of the tower, from which a length of cord was hanging; above, in the sky, he saw the flock of cawing crows.

Christian Bach told George Dubb that he recognised, with a starting of terror, that the length of cord was a twisted piece of the material from which Idilia's dress was made; he guessed that she had had the idea of using it to lower herself down to the heap of wooden rubble, but had not had the strength left to carry out the idea. Since he was unable to reach the length of cloth by stretching up his hand, Christian piled up pieces of rubble onto the heap on which he was standing, calling out Idilia's name all the while but receiving no answer.

Feeling overwhelmed with despair, but at the same time feeling there might still be a hope that he would find his beloved alive, Christian finally succeeded in grabbing hold of the piece of cloth, by stretching up with both hands from where he stood swaying on rotten planks and beams. Mustering every ounce of strength in his body Bach managed to pull himself up to the opening so that he could look over the edge.

The first thing he saw was Idilia's straw hat and shoes, lying on the platform at the top of the tower. Holding tightly onto the length of cloth he turned to look in the other direction, and his eyes fell on a sight that made him stiffen with dread and despair: lying on the grass-covered platform, close up against the tower wall, Idilia was lying as if asleep, her right arm extended towards the opening. On the back of the emaciated, naked girl there sat a crow, pecking at the body.

Christian told the shaken George Dubb that he had shouted and roared to scare away the crow and the other birds circling above, after which deathly silence had enveloped the tower. He had then shattered the silence with a scream filled with all his anguish and despair.

In order to reach Idilia's hand, on which she was wearing his crystal ring, he let go of the length of cloth with his right hand and stretched out towards the dead girl – but was unable to reach far enough. The length of cloth, to which he was clinging with his left hand, broke and with a cry Christian plunged down inside the tower. He landed on the heap of rotten timber, which gave way with a loud crashing noise. The fall broke his leg, and, bleeding from several wounds, he found himself buried beneath the rubble.

After spending half a day under the pile of old planks he managed to free himself, although he could not remember what had happened. Christian's experiences at the tower had left him in a state of traumatic shock, and it was not until weeks later that he could recollect what had induced this condition in him. Tortured by feelings of guilt and self-reproach, believing that he was responsible for Idilia's death, he had kept his knowledge of her tragic fate to himself, and tried to force it out of his consciousness by turning to hard physical labour in the mines of the Rhineland region – although a long time had to pass before he was able to get over his feeling of guilt.

In the summer of 1860, when for the first time Christian was no longer plagued by remorse at the death of Idilia and had even tentatively started making plans for the future, he suffered a reverse when Idilia's remains were discovered in the tower of the ruined castle of Lahneck. Suddenly all the memories and feelings of guilt came flooding back to him, and it felt as if he would break into pieces under their weight. With the aim of releasing this inner pressure he decided he would come forth and tell the people of the Rhineland his secret, and he was prepared to take any consequences this step might have. However, the unexpected appearance of George Dubb in Braubach had delayed the execution of his resolution. Surrendering to his fate, and desiring to pay his last respects to Idilia, Christian had come to the memorial service held at the Church of St Martin in honour of his beloved.

After listening to Christian Bach's story outside the church, George Dubb forgave the unhappy German for his years of silence regarding Idilia's whereabouts and advised him, since he in no way was responsible for Idilia's death, to keep his secret, and for the sake of peace not to tell any living person what he knew. George Dubb assured Christian that he would not even tell Idilia's mother the tragic circumstances surrounding Idilia's death, whereupon Christian, grateful for her brother's discretion, promised that he would not breathe any word on the subject.

When George Dubb said that he and his mother would be returning by steamer from Coblenz to England the very next day and would be taking the mortal remains of Idilia home with them, Christian Bach broke into tears. He brought his weeping under control, however, on catching sight of Elizabeth Dubb as she came out of the church. After greeting her briefly, and repeating his belated condolences, Christian hastily said farewell to them both and disappeared into the throng of people outside the church. Since it would be complicated and arduous to transport a coffin to Scotland via steam-ship and railway, George Dubb ordered a small, longish wooden box to be made by a carpenter in the town, in which it would be easier to transport the remains of his sister.

That evening in the Church of St Martin, the reverend Jakob Mohr and George Dubb laid the bones in the new wooden box, in the presence of Elizabeth Dubb. A sexton nailed the coffin shut, whereafter for additional security three leather straps were bound around it, before the priest blessed it.

The following morning at 9am in Coblenz, George Dubb and his mother boarded a steamer which was to take them, via Wesel, to Rotterdam. They kept with them in the cabin they were sharing the oblong wooden chest containing Idilia's mortal remains.

Half an hour later, shortly before the vessel was due to depart, George and Elizabeth Dubb, who were standing at the rail, were astonished to see Christian Bach board the ship. He was followed by two rather elderly male porters, who were dragging a leather armchair between them. Bach instructed them to take the armchair to the foredeck, and having carried out this direction the two men left the ship. Christian then asked the Dubbs if they could see their way to doing him a favour; and shortly afterwards, as the vessel steamed down the Rhine, Christian Bach sat in his leather armchair on the foredeck, holding the wooden chest containing Idilia Dubb's mortal remains in his lap.

He remained seated thus until, at 7pm, the boat reached Wesel; here, he returned the wooden chest to George and Elizabeth Dubb, left the vessel, and was never seen again. Two months later, a good while after Idilia had been buried in Edinburgh, her mother found on her daughter's grave a "Bad Emser" mineral water jar in which there was a single red rose.

In the summer of 1863 Idilia's sister, the 22-year-old Mary Dubb, travelled with a ship of a Dutch steam-ship company to Oberlahnstein. Among her travelling effects she had the water jar found on her sister's final resting place, filled with earth from the grave.

Being unable to locate Christian Bach, Mary betook herself early one morning to the now partially rebuilt Lahneck Castle and climbed up the tower at the top of which her sister had met her death. On reaching the top Mary scattered the earth from her sister's graveyard over the platform. The following morning she returned to the tower and did not leave the castle before twilight. She maintained this pattern for three days, then boarded a steamer and returned home to Scotland.

After the death of their mother five years later Mary and George Dubb emigrated to America, and all trace of them was lost.

Of the three friends who went out into the world in search of fame – Gwendolyn, Genevieve and Idilia – only Idilia made her name. The whole of Germany knew her story as that of "the English Fräulein", and she became known throughout the world as "the Scottish girl who vanished".

AFTERWORD
LONDON, JULY 1878

The "Diary of Miss Idilia", edited by Idilia Dubb's friend Genevieve Hill, never appeared in its entirety or in book-form; Idilia's parents allowed no more than short extracts to be published in the English and German press, owing to the negative picture their daughter had painted of them in the journal. It was not until July 1868, when both of Idilia's parents had died, that Genevieve Hill, now working as a librarian in London, received from Idilia's brother and sister written permission to offer the edited diary to a British publishing house. In August of that year George and Mary Dubb emigrated to America, leaving their sister's diary at Genevieve Hill's free disposal.

A few months later, following a riding accident which left her wheelchair-bound for the rest of her life, Genevieve returned to Edinburgh, and soon once more found work as a librarian. In her spare time she worked as a proof-reader for a Scottish newspaper publisher, and tried to write an adventure story. Finding herself unable to write a book, Genevieve decided to try and find a publisher for Idilia's diary. However, when the first publisher she offered the book to turned it down she gave up and made no further attempt to see it into print.

Soon the diary, and its author Idilia Dubb, were forgotten; scarcely anyone remembered the girl and the account she had given of her adventure-filled journey along the Rhine. Genevieve Hill's memories of Idilia faded as time went by, and the diary was left unread on a bookshelf to gather dust.

Another friend, whom Genevieve had by this time all but completely forgotten, was Gwendolyn O'Hara, who had emigrated to America with her parents years before. In spring 1879 Genevieve was surprised to receive a letter from her, in which she learnt that her friend no longer had any contact with her parents and was living in California. Gwendolyn wrote that she had long since abandoned her dream of a successful career as an opera or musical singer and now worked in San Francisco as a singer in saloons.

This unexpected letter from America marked the starting point of a long and intensive correspondence between the two Scottish women; in their letters they complained at how hard fate had been to them. In her final letter Gwendolyn announced that she would soon be returning to Edinburgh – but this was not to be: in October 1879 she died in San Francisco from a haemorrhage of the lungs, and was buried in a graveyard in that city.

When, months later, Genevieve Hill received a letter from Gwendolyn's parents informing her of their daughter's death, she fell into a deep depression and lost her will to live. She was taken in by her married sister, Betty McGregor, who lived in Glasgow, but she died of a heart attack in May 1880.

Following Genevieve's death her letters, and Idilia Dubb's diary, passed into the possession of the McGregor family; they were passed down to the family's children and grandchildren, until in 1951 they became the property of a private trust in Scotland.

In 1995 an American author, carrying out research for an historical novel to be based in the Rhineland, came across the article printed in the *Adenauer Kreis-und Wochenblatt* newspaper on 26 October 1863, which recounted the tragic fate that had befallen Idilia Dubb. Fascinated, the American set out to track down her diary, a quest which led him from the Rhineland to England, and thence to Scotland. Initially, the trust's administrators refused to release it for publication, citing Idilia's parents, who had not wanted to allow the diary to be published 145 years previously. When however they were shown a document in which George and Mary Dubb clearly stated that they had no objection to the book's being published, the administrators yielded and, in return for a commensurate fee, allowed themselves to be persuaded to make "The Diary of Miss Idilia" available to a wider public.

The publication of this book brings this intention to realisation.

Due to the mysterious circumstances in which this diary was found, its authenticity can never be entirely verified. What is certain is that a young girl did disappear while on holiday with her family in the Coblenz region in 1851. Her diary, apparently found at the scene of her death, garnered immediate widespread interest and, although several people over the years have sought to disprove its veracity, no one has yet succeeded.